1913

Oliver DeMille

First Edition, July 2012

ISBN: 978-0-9853387-6-3
LCCN: 2012911659

Published by:
Obstaclés Press Inc.
4072 Market Place Dr.
Flint, MI 48507

Cover design and layout by Norm Williams - nwa-inc.com
Edited by Stephen Palmer

Printed in the United States of America

It is necessary always to give a great deal of thought to liberty. There is no substitute for it. Nothing else is quite so effective. Unless it be preserved, there is little else that is worthwhile...The protection of rights is righteous. —Calvin Coolidge

TABLE OF CONTENTS

FOREWORD

Oliver DeMille is uniquely qualified to share the Turning Points of Freedom. As a lifelong scholar, author, and educator, he has been on the front lines for almost two decades, protecting American freedoms through his teachings and writings. DeMille has authored numerous top-selling books, including the widely-acclaimed *A Thomas Jefferson Education*.

When I first met Oliver, I was impressed by his wide range of readings, near-photographic recall of thousands of books and writings, and passion for liberty. In fact, I believe DeMille is one of the most honest, intelligent, and capable patriots in America today.

After an enjoyable, nearly all-day discussion together, I asked him where things went wrong with freedom. He immediately responded, "1913."

I smiled because my readings pointed to the same thing. We discussed changes by the Supreme Court during Jefferson's presidency, alterations to the system during and after the Civil War, and the changes brought by the Progressive Era. After another few hours of conversation, he cemented his outline of this book *1913*.

Acting on his inspired clarity, DeMille pounded out this masterpiece in near-record time. I believe this book will be one of his all-time best sellers, mainly because it captures so succinctly the decline of Western Civilization and the high point in American freedom along with its potential resurgence.

In our many conversations since that first meeting, we have discussed numerous important events and characters from the history of freedom. We have talked about concepts taught in Gibbon's *The Decline and Fall of the Roman Empire*, decisions made by Abraham Lincoln and Winston Churchill, thought leaders from Burke and Jefferson to Ray Kroc and Sam Walton, the deep economic principles in Ludwig Von Mises' book *Human Action*, how the Federalist/Anti-Federalist debate is still relevant today, the huge (albeit little-known) influence of Buckminster Fuller, the merits and flaws of various potential changes to the American system, and many other topics of freedom and leadership through human history. But our conversations have frequently come back to the vital impact of 1913.

What makes the year 1913 so unique? What actually happened to freedom in 1913? And how have these events altered the freedoms for people living in North America? DeMille's new book shows that every few generations, society goes through what he calls a "World Shift" and that each shift moves civilization either in the direction of freedom or in the direction of force. In *1913*, DeMille pinpoints the Turning Points that occurred when four vital checks were removed from the Constitution. The four Turning Points Oliver details are painful enough on their own, but disastrous when combined.

Originally, the United States Constitution was written to grant enough power to government while serving as an effective check on too much centralized power, limiting government's field of operation. However, due to misinterpretations and misapplications of the founders' words and intentions, today's federal government operates well outside these intended boundaries. The changes that occurred in 1913 were among the worst such moves away from the system of freedom outlined by the American framers and established, through much pain and sacrifice, by the founding generations. The result was a government that is increasingly beyond the control of the American people.

America must turn away from the precipice and engage the path of freedom—and reading *1913* is a great first step. More than detailing specific events, DeMille's book reveals what freedom truly is, why it is so vital, how it is being lost, and how regular people can take action to ensure we pass on the blessings of liberty and prosperity to our posterity.

DeMille not only tells us how 1913 was the Turning Point away from freedom, but he also does so much more: He shows us how another Turning Point is coming and how it will either move us even further away from freedom or turn us strongly back in the direction of freedom. He also explains how a certain group of people are going to make this decision and teaches us the three things each of us can do to become part of this powerful group. He outlines how realistic these things are and helps us get started.

This isn't a doomsday book, but rather a primer on how we can realistically restore and promote freedom. DeMille shows us how to become better leaders and to really make a significant difference in the future of our prosperity and freedom. This is a book about freedom, family, business, prosperity, and leadership—and about how all of these go together in a free society.

You're holding a masterpiece on freedom, and everyone who cares about the future of prosperity and freedom should read and apply this book.

—**Orrin Woodward**, *Best-Selling Author and Recipient of the 2011 Independent Association of Businesses' Top Leader of the Year Award*

The Year That Changed Everything

The year was 1913.

Most Americans still owned farms or shops, while many worked in factories and belonged to unions. The great tradition of threading the May Pole in Central Park was in full swing. Most little cities and towns had similar unique holidays and traditional celebrations.

Horses were everywhere—in the cities, the towns, and in the backyard of every home. Machinery was on the rise, however, and threatened to revolutionize everything soon.

Henry Ford created a new business model as he wrote a speech on profit sharing for Ford Motor Company. Ty Cobb was thrilling baseball audiences. A racially-charged debate raged in Washington about immigration—whether Irish, Jewish, and Italian immigrants should be stopped at the borders.

The first Charlie Chaplin movies came out, and two future classics were published: *O Pioneers!* by Willa Cather and *Pollyanna* by Eleanor Porter. The Grand Central Station terminal in New York City was completed, and the foxtrot came into fashion.

In Europe, a revolution in art was adding a number of new names to the lexicon—cubism, expressionism, and futurism—while in America, a transformation in architecture was under way in the designs of Frank Lloyd Wright. Filmmakers were pioneering new technologies, and for the first time, businessmen began using film in the workplace (by recording factory workers and analyzing the efficiency of their work and systems).

A little-known diplomat named Lewis Einstein warned in *The National Review* that the rise of Germany would be a major threat to Britain and America for decades to come. He went so far as to say that America was vulnerable to attack by Germany or its allies and to warn her (basically in vain) to prepare.

Many noticed that technology was creating changes, but few people knew how big 1913 would be in the history of the world. In the midst of all this economic and technological change, a newly-elected president of the United States sat down and wrote a speech.

Wilson's Portentous Speech

When President Woodrow Wilson gave his inaugural address on March 4, few realized how far-reaching his words would be. Mortimer Adler wrote in *The Annals of America* that Wilson's address is often "compared to Jefferson's first and Lincoln's second" inaugural for its lasting impact on the nation.

Wilson said that his administration was a time for change. He said that Washington, D.C., had long adopted a "hands-off" philosophy of maintaining national security and law enforcement, leaving people otherwise to their own devices, but that it was time to use the federal government in many other ways.

This turned out to be a blueprint for America ever since. And 1913, the same year Wilson gave his speech, was the Turning Point *away* from American freedom. Three major events in 1913, and another corresponding event in 1936, together created the biggest Turning Point of Freedom in modern times.

> *1913 was the Turning Point* away *from American freedom.*

Few people in America or the world understood the import of Wilson's speech or these world-altering events as they occurred. It appears that more people took notice of Ty Cobb and May Pole celebrations around the nation than of these critical events.

Unfortunately, the same thing frequently happens today; important events occur while few people take notice. Hopefully, an understanding of 1913 will help us be better citizens and leaders in our time and encourage us to pay closer attention to the proposals and documents in our day that will likely make a huge impact on world events.

As direct results of these events, American citizens now pay much higher taxes, fight with burdensome and costly regulations, and enjoy much less freedom. Because of these events, the rich get richer, the poor get poorer, and the middle class has less social mobility than ever before. Because of these events, America's freedom, prosperity, power, and influence continue to decrease while she increases her spending and debt. Washington is broken, Congress flounders, and special interests rule because of these events.

Let me make this as clear and concrete as possible: Today, you work longer and harder for less benefit, your money buys less and less with each passing year, you have a decreased chance of becoming financially independent, you have less say in government policy and direction, the federal government and elitists have more power over your every-day decisions, and your life is more complicated *precisely because of the combined effect of these events*. You pay more for bread, milk, eggs, shoes, gasoline, and everything else. You have a harder time starting a business and making it profitable. You have more red tape to cut through and higher fees to pay when you build a house. Your health care costs have skyrocketed, and your choices have diminished.

These events are not footnotes in history textbooks; they have a direct, significant, and negative impact on virtually every aspect of your daily life. They have far more impact on your life than any current election. Indeed, they largely determine the results of today's elections.

What About Solutions?

When asked what is needed to get America back on track, a wide variety of answers can be given.

A large part of the problem is that few Americans know where things went wrong. Without knowing the origin and source of the infection, without an understanding of the Turning Point of Freedom—the three events of 1913 and the follow-up event of 1936—they are unable to diagnose the real problem. Thus, we remain deeply divided on what the solutions should be.

Few people have ever heard about these four events on the nightly news or in the mass media. Nor are these events widely talked about in our schools. Indeed, when they are infrequently mentioned in modern times, it is usually in an angry and extremist tone that strikes us as desperate and unconstructive.

Still, three significant events occurred in 1913, which led to a fourth event in 1936. Together these created a Turning Point away from the American success formula of freedom, free enterprise, and widespread economic opportunity.

Until we understand these events, it is difficult, if not impossible, to understand how similar changes in our time could take us back in the direction of freedom—or to agree on what such changes should be.

Once we do understand these events, there are clear and practical solutions, and *you* can and must be on the front lines of enacting them. Specifically, America needs you to become 1) a successful entrepreneur, 2) a voracious reader and independent thinker, and 3) a "tribal" leader. By the time you're done reading this book, you'll understand how those three solutions correspond with the events I'll detail. You'll also understand exactly how to live them powerfully to impact freedom. In short, you'll know how to make life better for yourself and your posterity.

High Stakes

Freedom matters. Freedom includes political freedom, spiritual freedom, and financial freedom, and a decrease in any one of these leads to a decrease in all. Without real freedom, our posterity will have less opportunity and a lower standard of living.

> *Freedom matters.*

At some point, each of us in the current generation will have to look our grandchildren in the eyes. We will have to either tell them we sat back and watched as their freedoms were eroded or that we played an active, significant role in creating the great return to freedom that they enjoy. It is up to us.

In *Federalist Paper* 1, Alexander Hamilton wrote, "It has been frequently remarked that it seems to have been reserved to the people of this country, by their conduct and example, to decide the important question, whether societies of men are really capable or not of establishing good government from reflection and choice, or whether they are forever destined to depend for their political constitutions on accident and force."

In similar fashion, our generation will determine whether the American Dream continues or becomes a thing of mere history. As throughout history, a few small things will determine which direction our society takes during our generation—toward freedom or away from it. Elections can help our society, but without a few key changes, our elections won't bring the results we need. And until enough citizens understand what these changes are and how to enact them, America will continue to decline.

To understand how a few small events change everything, and to make the right choices about the small things of our time that will bring massive change, American citizens must understand the last critical Turning Point of Freedom: 1913.

CHAPTER 1

The Turning Point of Freedom

"We review the past not in order that we return to it but that we may find in what direction, straight and clear, it points to the future."
—Calvin Coolidge

Some small events are so significant that they sway everything that comes later. Such events include the abduction of Helen and the resulting Trojan War, the trial of Socrates in Athens, the murder of Caesar, the fall of Rome, the rise of Martin Luther, the journey of Columbus, the sailing of the *Mayflower*, the Boston Tea Party, the election of Abraham Lincoln, the bombing of Pearl Harbor, the assassination of John F. Kennedy, and the terrorist attacks of 9/11, among others.

Some of these world-changing events bring good consequences for society, leading to increased opportunity, freedom, and prosperity. Others cause a loss of freedom and bring many negatives to the world. Either way, such events are Turning Points. Once they occur, they impact the future in surprising ways that create lasting changes.

The Turning Point of the American Founding

America was founded as the result of three such world-altering events:

1. The Boston Tea Party, which led to the American Revolution
2. The writing of *The Declaration of Independence,* which set the tone for the expansion and growth of a nation dedicated to the idea that "all men are created equal"
3. The establishment of the United States Constitution, which created a new nation and gave it the strength to grow and flourish in an environment of freedom and widespread prosperity

These three changes guided the direction of the United States for over a century afterwards.

A fourth change, seemingly small at the time but with huge consequences over the course of the nineteenth century, was the adoption of the Monroe Doctrine. In this document, which came thirty-one years after the ratification of the U.S. Constitution (and as a direct result of it), the United States kept the colonial powers of Europe from carving up the territory of the Western Hemisphere and making it subservient to the aristocratic families of Europe that dominated most of Africa, Asia, Oceania, and the Middle East.

Without these four turning-point events, the history of America and the entire world would be very different. For nearly a century, these four events helped shape the development of America and the ideas of freedom, free enterprise, and widespread prosperity.

Unfortunately, another major Turning Point came in 1913. This time, three significant world-changing events all occurred during the same year. Any of the three alone would have been a drastic blow to freedom. But together, the result was a disaster.

We are still experiencing the consequences of this change. In fact, the three events of 1913 created so many problems for freedom and prosperity that we can refer to them collectively as the Turning Point of Freedom.

Similar to the American founding era, a fourth event came a few years later and became part of this negative Turning Point. The three disturbing changes of 1913 actually catalyzed the fourth harmful event twenty-three years later in 1936, just as the three events of the American founding directly influenced the adoption of the Monroe Doctrine in 1820.

The American Dream

The great freedom model created by the American founders unleashed liberty on a growing populace and allowed them to use free enterprise to create the most wealthy and powerful nation in history.

Over time, this formula helped correct many of its own internal weaknesses, including the spread of freedom to all races, both gen-ders, and many people around the world. Moreover, under this American success formula, freedom and wealth were widespread throughout the people at all economic levels rather than centralized in a few powerful aristo-cratic families. This environment of liberty, enterprise, and abundant opportunity came to be known as the American Dream.

> *The great freedom model created by the American founders unleashed liberty on a growing populace and allowed them to use free enterprise to create the most wealthy and powerful nation in history.*

As Cleon Skousen documented in *The Making of America*, using this formula of freedom, by the year 1945 Americans, with only 6 percent of the world's population, were producing over half of the world's goods, services, and wealth. The American people under this system of freedom enjoyed the highest standard of living in world history.

America had the most successful and free system in the entire world, and American generations newly born looked forward to the same opportunities in the decades and centuries ahead. Immigrants from around the world flocked to the United States—often in the face of major hardship and sacrifice—seeking the same benefits.

Seeds of Decline

Unfortunately by 1945, the seeds of decline were already beginning to sprout. The four events of 1913 and 1936 had already been put in motion. For a time, freedom would continue to flourish even as these enemies of liberty and prosperity began to mature and expand. But eventually, Americans everywhere would start to feel the forces of decline.

In our post-9/11 world, the weakening of the American Dream is a reality seen and felt by everyone. Nearly all Americans now sense something is wrong, that changes are needed, and that Washington can't (or won't) fix it. People put renewed hope in each election, but they are routinely disappointed after the elections are over.

Pundits debate about whether the federal government is broken, while citizens join various political or social movements in the hope of somehow returning our nation to its former level of freedom and opportunity. Some blame the government; others hold a certain party responsible for the national downturn, while still others affix the blame to Wall Street greed, Hollywood smut, or some other symptom of decline.

Others, most notably the scholar Joseph S. Nye, argue that we are not actually in decline but rather just addicted to some bad policies. For most Americans, it still feels like decline—whatever the experts want to call it.

More and more Americans now feel that without significant changes in our society, their children will have less opportunity and a lower standard of living than they did—and that the children in China will have more prosperity than America's rising generations.

Everyone Knows

Americans are aware—either directly or indirectly—of what the leading journalists and experts are saying. For example, Ian Bremmer and Nouriel Roubini wrote in the March/April 2011 issue of *Foreign Affairs* that in the post-financial crisis world, the United States is no longer the leader of the global economy and that no other nation has the ability to replace it.

Former Reagan speech writer Peggy Noonan wrote in *The Wall Street Journal* (October 27, 2005) that many people in our current society have a sense that "the wheels are coming off the trolley and the trolley off the tracks" and that many who have the means are preparing their finances and holdings for major downturns ahead.

Researchers William Strauss and Neil Howe wrote in their book *The Fourth Turning* that, "Wherever we're headed, America is evolving in ways most of us don't like or understand. Individually focused yet collectively adrift, we wonder if we're headed toward a waterfall . . . a decisive era of secular upheaval, when the values regime propels the replacement of the old civic order with a new one."

David Brooks wrote in *The New York Times* (November 11, 2010) that the U.S. is headed toward bankruptcy and that by 2020, we will be spending $1 trillion annually just on the interest of our national debt. He said that at some point before then, a "catastrophe" will come and that the ensuing financial shock will be humiliating and cause drastic cuts and pain.

Niall Ferguson wrote in *Newsweek* (November 27, 2009) that we are following the path of declining empires and that such decline begins with an explosion in debt.

Journalist Thomas Friedman wrote in *The New York Times* (June 29, 2008) that the U.S. is a nation in decline and that our government seems incapable of solving our biggest problems or engaging our biggest opportunities. He also noted (January 30, 2010) that international business leaders are beginning to see the United States as unstable and unpredictable—a concept usually reserved, Friedman said, for nations like Russia, Iran, or Honduras.

In 2010, Larry King cited a CNN Opinion Research Poll which asked people if the federal government has become so big that it is a threat to our rights and freedoms. Fifty-six percent of Americans polled said "yes."

Joseph S. Nye, Jr., pointed out in *Foreign Affairs* (November/December 2010) that 61 percent of Americans in a Pew Research Center poll said the U.S. is in decline, and a mere 19 percent trust the government to do the right thing most of the time. He noted that in 1964, three-quarters of Americans thought the federal government would do the right thing most of the time.

Joe Klein wrote in *Time* (October 7, 2010) that many Americans are deeply concerned about the rise of China and the simultaneous mediocrity of the United States.

Such concerns about America's declining place in the world, especially about its struggling economy, and what this means for the future are now commonplace in our national dialogue.

American Decline

In his book *RESOLVED: 13 Resolutions for LIFE*, Orrin Woodward summarized the Five Laws of Decline from Edward Gibbon's
classic *The Decline and Fall of the Roman Empire*. Woodward wrote
that, according to Gibbon, there are "...five attributes that marked
the Roman Empire at the time of its fall over 1,500 years ago:

A mounting love of show and luxury (affluence)

A widening gap between the very rich and the very poor

An obsession with sex

Freakishness in the arts, masquerading as originality

An increased desire to live off the state."

Certainly we see these in our current society. Woodward continued:
"Indeed, a solid argument could be made that the modern West has
surpassed Rome in many of its negative influences."

A large majority of Americans agree that something is wrong in
America. They see it on the news, they experience it in their every-
day careers and families, and they feel that it may be getting worse.
Few will even argue anymore about whether America is headed in
the wrong direction.

The question is: *Where* did we go wrong, and *how* do we fix it? It
all started in 1913.

CHAPTER 2

World-Shifting Event #1: The Sixteenth Amendment

"Perfection of means and confusion of
goals seem to characterize our age."
—Albert Einstein

The first major turning-point event of 1913 was the passage of the Sixteenth Amendment to the Constitution.

Before this amendment, the federal government got a large portion of its tax money directly from state governments as outlined in the Constitution. This created a natural check on the federal government by the states because Washington depended on the states for its funding. Washington would have no recourse if the states were to refuse to fund the budget. It could argue, vote, issue executive orders, and deliver Supreme Court decisions, but if the states stood firm together, the federal government would eventually have to give in to the states or lose its funding.

Once the Sixteenth Amendment was in place, however, this all changed. In fact, it reversed. Now the states are dependent on Washington for much of their funding. In our day, state governments routinely give in to federal demands in order to keep the money flowing.

> Now the states are dependent on Washington for much of their funding. In our day, state governments routinely give in to federal demands in order to keep the money flowing.

In *Federalist Papers* 18-20, James Madison showed how important it is for the federal government to have independent powers rather than be dependent on the states for everything. He used history to demonstrate that federal dependency on the states would make the nation weak, as shown in all historical examples including many Greek city-states, the German nations, and other European governments. But the states must not become totally dependent on the central government either.

Hamilton wrote in *Federalist* 32 that even though the federal government would raise some taxes directly, it would get most of its monies from the states and would never tax too much anyway because the Constitution doesn't allow Washington to spend for anything except the twenty powers outlined in Article I, Section 8.

Clearly, this didn't turn out the way Hamilton expected. Once the states lost their tax-check on Washington, they were unable to stand independently against the federal government on funding issues. As a result of the Sixteenth Amendment, the United States became less of a federal system (where the states together form a power equal to that of Washington) and more of a national model (with the states being subordinate to Washington).

Direct vs. Indirect Taxation

Note that, for the framers, the question of taxes was among the most important facets of the new Constitution. For example, of the eighty-five *Federalist Papers*, fully twelve of them were addressed specifically to how federal taxation would work—more than any other single topic covered in the *Federalist*.

> *As a result of the Sixteenth Amendment, the United States became less of a federal system (where the states together form a power equal to that of Washington) and more of a national model (with the states being subordinate to Washington).*

The major point of the authors of the *Federalist* was that the federal government could only use indirect taxes with people, never direct taxes. The difference between these two is mostly lost on modern Americans, but it is vital to freedom.

A direct tax is one where the entity that gets to *spend* the tax money gets it directly from the entity *paying* the tax. An indirect tax is one where the entity that will spend the tax revenue gets it through an intermediary.

For example, income tax is paid directly from the individual or business to the federal government. This is a direct tax.

In contrast, sales tax is paid to the state government, but the consumer pays the tax to a business when a purchase is made. Therefore, sales taxes are collected and submitted to the government by businesses, and the consumer never has to deal directly with a state official. This is what makes the tax *indirect*.

This was an important distinction for the American framers because they had experienced much abuse in the British system of direct taxation. They saw numerous agents and agencies of the British government abuse power in their interactions with taxpayers. In response, they wanted the American system to be different. Specifically, they never wanted agents of the federal government to have direct power over American taxpayers. Thus, they pushed strongly for indirect taxes, where the taxpayers would pay their taxes to the state government, which would serve as a buffer between the citizens and the federal government.

Part of this was the principle of avoiding a conflict of interest. This means that when the entity that gets to keep and spend the tax money also has the power to directly collect it from the citizen, it will naturally be less fair than a third party which collects the tax but doesn't get to keep it. When this conflict of interest is removed, freedom increases.

The Irish vs. Scottish Models

Beyond these very important technical considerations of freedom, the framers had deep and important reasons for wanting the states to collect the taxes needed federally and for blocking the federal government from collecting taxes directly from individuals or businesses. This principle was rooted in their study of history, and they felt strongly about it based on their experiences in the Revolutionary War against Britain.

An important part of this understanding came from the history of Scotland versus that of Ireland. Nearly all in the founding generation studied this history, and they knew that the power of taxation and how it is collected has a direct and lasting impact on freedom. By the time of the American founding, both Scotland and Ireland had long been part of the

> *The power of taxation and how it is collected has a direct and lasting impact on freedom.*

British Empire, but the experiences of these two nations were very different.

Scotland answered to Britain but had its own parliament and paid taxes to the Scottish leaders, who then sent their required amount to the British crown. This protected the Scottish people from the excesses of British government agents, military recruiters, and tax collectors. Scots did fight a number of battles with Britain over time. But through the course of many centuries, this protection from Britain by the Scottish government provided the Scots with a great deal of freedom and prosperity not often enjoyed by other British colonies.

Ireland, on the other hand, suffered mercilessly because its people answered directly to the British parliament. The Irish people paid their taxes directly to British agents and were subjected to arrests, intrusions, and collection of their private papers and records without warrant any time a government officer wanted to make things difficult for them. This led to many abuses, and over time, the Irish were seen as the lowest people in the British class system.

An American Response

The Americans knew this history of Scotland and Ireland, and they were determined not to follow the course of Ireland. In fact, as British abuses grew before the Revolutionary War, many American leaders argued that America should remain part of the British Empire and subject to the King as long as each American colony was governed by its own parliament. But when the British parliament required a tax on tea in America—a direct national tax that ignored the votes of the colonial parliament—the Americans revolted in the Boston Tea Party. While Americans were willing to be subject to Britain in the Scottish tradition, they refused to follow the pattern of Ireland. This led to the *Declaration of Independence* and the War of Independence.

After losing many friends and family members fighting the war, not to mention homes and businesses, Americans didn't want the states to follow the Irish pattern with a new federal government. In fact, without the prohibition against direct federal taxes on the income and assets of individuals and businesses (in Article I, Section 9), the American people would not have ratified the Constitution. It meant that much to them.

They didn't want to be slaves to Washington like the Irish people had become enslaved to London. They explicitly wanted to be independent in each state following the Scottish model. Thus, the founding generation chose to only allow state governments to directly tax, and they kept the power of the federal government at bay by not allowing it to collect direct taxes.

> *The founding generation chose to only allow state governments to directly tax, and they kept the power of the federal government at bay by not allowing it to collect direct taxes.*

More than a Technicality

This wasn't just a technicality for them. They believed that giving the central government power over direct taxation was an attack on freedom. History had borne this out, and they knew their history.

In our time, the concept is hardly considered important by most Americans, much less a matter of deep and passionate debate. When a candidate does argue for a specific kind of taxation or a different tax policy in our modern world, most Americans tune it out. They don't understand what all the fuss is about. They wonder why the candidate is so passionate about such a technical, wonky topic and often make him out to be an extremist.

Those who have closely studied the history of freedom, however, have

> *In practical application, few issues matter more to freedom than tax policy.*

a very different reaction. In practical application, few issues matter more to freedom than tax policy, and the Sixteenth Amendment started a massive shift away from the free system the founders established.

Most people wouldn't agree to let somebody else take money from them on terms they didn't understand if they were going into business or buying a product or service. And although it may seem tedious or impractical, we as citizens need to realize that it is our job to understand tax policy and to work toward policies that are principled, wise, just, and sustainable.

With the tax policies in place in our current law, it is important that citizens pay their legal taxes. Otherwise, they disqualify themselves from taking part in the process that can restore good government, and the downward spiral will continue. It is also vital for good citizens to understand these issues and help elect officials who will move America toward a better tax system.

The Constitution made it illegal in Article I, Section 9 for the federal government to collect direct taxes except in extreme cases, and numerous commentaries in the *Federalist Papers* discussed why indirect taxes are key to freedom and direct taxes are dangerous.

The *Federalist* Speaks Out

In *Federalist* 21, for example, Alexander Hamilton argued that it is fine for the federal government to assess direct taxes on the state governments, but not on individuals or businesses. This is spelled out specifically in Article I, Section 2 of the U.S. Constitution. Under this system, the amount the federal government needed was determined, and then the amount was divided among the states according to their populations. This was called apportionment. The federal government apportioned the amount it needed and collected it directly from the states. But all taxes from the federal government on businesses and individuals had to be indirect.

In *Federalist* 33, Hamilton also taught that leaving direct taxes to the power of the states (and not the federal government) is an important check on the power of the federal government and that if the federal government could get its money directly from the people that it would both decrease the freedom of the people and negatively impact the sovereign powers of the states.

The Twenty Enumerated Powers of the Federal Government

James Madison taught in *Federalist* 41 that the government could only tax in order to spend on things approved in the Constitution. In other words, no money could be spent (and no taxes raised) for things outside of or beyond the following twenty powers outlined in Article I, Section 8:

1.   Regulate commerce
2.   Establish rules for citizenship
3.   Establish bankruptcy laws

4. Coin and regulate the value of money

5. Standardize weights and measures

6. Punish counterfeiting

7. Run a postal system

8. Pass copyright and patent laws

9. Run federal courts

10. Punish crimes on the high seas

11. Declare war

12. Raise and finance the armed forces

13. Establish rules for the armed forces

14. Call up state militias

15. Administer the seat of government (Washington, D.C.)

16. Administer federal lands

17. Pass laws to implement the other items on this list

18. Raise tax money to pay for the other items on this list

19. Spend it on the other items on this list

20. Borrow if needed to pay for the items on this list

These are the only powers given the federal government by the Constitution and the only things the federal government is constitutionally authorized to spend money on. Of course, if today's government stuck to this list, our problems of national debt, deficits, unbalanced budgets, bloated spending, and big government would disappear almost immediately. But the turning-point events of 1913 and 1936 changed the federal limits of these twenty powers.

A Drastic Shift

The adoption of the Sixteenth Amendment started this drastic shift from these twenty powers to the thousands of things the federal government now does. Madison predicted in *Federalist* 41 that the American government would eventually be tempted to go beyond its twenty constitutional powers, and he pointed out in no uncertain terms that the federal government has no such legitimate powers under the Constitution.

> *The adoption of the Sixteenth Amendment started this drastic shift from these twenty powers to the thousands of things the federal government now does.*

The Supreme Court upheld this for over a century, including striking down the income tax law passed by Congress in 1894 as unconstitutional. Note that the tax in this law was actually very small—only a two percent flat tax on excess incomes of the very wealthy. Still, the court upheld the original intent of the framers that direct taxes on individuals or businesses are unconstitutional.

Only an amendment could change this original guarantee of American freedom from an over-spending government—and this is exactly what occurred with the passage of the Sixteenth Amendment.

Many have written about the history of this drastic change in the American system. Some have focused on the aristocratic forces that pushed for this from behind the scenes, and others have suggested that the amendment was never appropriately ratified. But regardless of such arguments, we have lived under the Sixteenth Amendment for a century now, and the results have been negative to American freedom and prosperity.

> *We have lived under the Sixteenth Amendment for a century now, and the results have been negative to American freedom and prosperity.*

But the Sixteenth Amendment wasn't the only loss of freedom that occurred in 1913.

CHAPTER 3

World-Shifting Event #2:
The Seventeenth Amendment

As with the Sixteenth Amendment, the Seventeenth Amendment continued the move away from states' rights and limited federal power.

Before this amendment, according to the Constitution, senators were selected from each state *according to the direction of the State Legislature.* This put two direct representatives of each respective state in Washington, with the power through checks and balances to protect the rights and interests of the states *themselves.*

Once the Seventeenth Amendment was implemented, however, senators were elected by popular vote within the states rather than by state legisla-

> *Once the Seventeenth Amendment was implemented, however, senators were elected by popular vote within the states rather than by state legislatures. This took the direct protectors of the states out of Washington.*

tures. This took the direct protectors of the states out of Washington.

This new method of electing senators affected how they tended to vote. Before the Seventeenth Amendment, it was mostly the members of the House of Representatives who tended to vote for increased spending programs. Since they were elected directly by the people, and since the people often wanted to have increased benefits from the government, it was natural that their interest was in voting for the programs that the people found tempting. By contrast, in the original model, senators tended to vote *against* increased spending proposals since they were elected by the state legislatures, which had to foot the bill of increased spending.

After the amendment was adopted, however, both representatives of the House and senators were now direct representatives of the people, and nobody represented the states, or the voice of frugality. Both the House and the Senate now tended to vote for increases. The natural check on spending disappeared.

> *The natural check on spending disappeared.*

Democracy vs. Aristocracy

Many people who read about the Seventeenth Amendment today jump to the conclusion that it actually helped freedom by making senators more responsive to the people. Indeed, the promoters of this amendment in 1913 made the same argument—that it would make America more democratic.

The reality is very different than the headline, however. While the direct election of senators may seem more democratic at first glance, a deeper analysis shows that it hurt American freedom.

The framers of the Constitution looked at the major forces of power in society and tried to make sure that the Constitution balanced and checked the power of each group. They wanted both the wealthy and the poor to have representation, and for neither to gain full control of the federal government.

They also wanted the federal and state levels of government to each have different powers and to check and balance each other so that neither the states nor the federal government could take power over the other.

The Seventeenth Amendment disrupted both of these balances and ended both of these checks on too much power. The states lost their control over the Senate, and as a result, the federal government slowly but surely took over many state powers. Today, nearly all Americans see the government in Washington, D.C., as above all the state governments— because this is the reality we live under. But it was not the original intent of the framers. We have lost many freedoms because of this change.

> *The states lost their control over the Senate, and as a result, the federal government slowly but surely took over many state powers.*

Government by Technocracy

On the issue of the wealthy losing their influence in the Senate, most people have a harder time seeing what happened. At first glance, it seems obvious that having the Senate answer to the regular people rather than aristocratic groups from each state benefits the nation.

But the founders saw this differently. For example, John Adams taught that a reduction of the wealth and influence of senators always leads to less natural power in the checks and balances of the Senate over the executive branch of government. When the Senate is made up mostly of the wealthy class, he said, the wealthy will seek this position of status and use it to keep the presidency in check. A Senate made up mostly of the wealthy classes from the states keeps the power of the presidency in line.

In contrast, when the Senate is like the House and elected by the popular vote, the wealthy classes will stop seeking the status of the Senate and instead put their efforts toward the presidency and serving in the executive branch. Or, for many of them, the incentive is to forego public service altogether, stay in the private sector as heads of business and industry, and use their wealth and influence to sway executive branch contracts toward their companies.

Additionally, in such a situation, the wealthy will typically use their wealth to take over the political parties, hire lobbyists, and establish special interest groups that promote their agendas behind the scenes. Such influence is out of the eye of most citizens but has huge control over government policies and actions.

In other words, we can choose a Senate where the most wealthy and influential characters in the nation are officially involved in legislation and on the public record, or a Senate that seems demo-cratic but leaves the most wealthy and influential characters in the nation out of the public eye yet consistently involved in unofficial governance. Again, John Adams outlined this reality long before our modern technological world even existed. In *A Defence of the Con-stitutions of the Government of the United States of America*, he wrote:

> The rich, the well-born, and the able, acquire an influ-ence among the people that will soon be too much for simple honesty and plain sense, in a house of representatives. The most illustrious of them must, therefore, be separated from the mass, and placed themselves in a Senate....
>
> A member of a Senate, of immense wealth, the most re-spected birth, and transcendent abilities, has no influence in the nation, in comparison of what he would have in a sin-gle representative assembly. When a Senate exists, the most powerful man in the state may be safely admitted into the House of Representatives, because the people have it in their power to remove him into the Senate as soon as his influence becomes dangerous.
>
> The Senate becomes the great object of ambition; and the richest and most sagacious wish to merit an advancement to it by services to the public in the house. When he has ob-tained the object of his wishes, you may still hope for the benefits of his exertions, without dreading his passions; for the executive power being in other hands, he has lost much

of his influence with the people, and can govern very few votes more than his own among the senators.

Founding Depth

The founding generation was widely read in the great classics of human history and the greatest political and economic thinkers of all time. They were close students of the government documents of history, and they put the Constitution together carefully and with precise purposes. When we change the Constitution, by amendment or by legislation, we need to be equally wise. We need to look through every detail and choose accordingly.

While the Seventeenth Amendment may appear more democratic to many onlookers, we need a deeper standard of analysis to really understand whether it is good or bad. Before the Seventeenth Amendment, the majority of powerful leaders in American history made their mark and pursued their goals and agendas on the public record—in the Senate or the White House.

Since 1913, such powerful individuals have been more prone to promote their goals and agendas from behind the scenes—influencing or simply purchasing media institutions, academic organizations, lobbying and special interest groups, political parties, and big business. The people have much less control over the actions and influences of men and women in associations, foundations, social marketing campaigns, or corporate and other private arenas of leadership than they did on senators prior to the Seventeenth Amendment.

In addition to changing how the federal government taxed people in the Sixteenth Amendment, the adoption of the Seventeenth Amendment shifted the focus of the Senate from being the center place of national frugality to becoming another parliamentary assembly bent on increasing taxes and spending more government money.

Taken together, the Sixteenth and Seventeenth Amendments effectively supported Wilson's move away from Jeffersonian government. The Sixteenth Amendment gave the national government more power to directly raise tax revenues, while the Seventeenth Amendment removed a natural thriftiness in the Senate and incentivized congressional leaders in both houses to spend more.

At the same time, these two amendments removed nearly all direct state representation in Washington and the constitutionally-established state checks on the federal government. As mentioned above, this in effect ended the equality of the states and the federal government and created a new American model with the national government in charge of subordinate states.

> *The Sixteenth Amendment gave the national government more power to directly raise tax revenues, while the Seventeenth Amendment removed a natural thriftiness in the Senate and incentivized congressional leaders in both houses to spend more.*

This is clearly not what the American founders had in mind. In fact, the writers of the *Federalist Papers* and also the *Anti-Federalist*

Papers were strongly against such a plan. In 1913, however, we made the shift.

After the Sixteenth and Seventeenth Amendments, the powers-that-be in 1913 were just getting started.

CHAPTER 4

World-Shifting Event #3: The Federal Reserve

The third turning-point event in 1913 was the establishment of the Federal Reserve. Again, this development was right in line with the goals of Wilson's speech: to move away from Jeffersonian limited government and toward a central government that does more and more.

In reality, the Federal Reserve was another National Bank of America, but the unpopularity of the earlier national banks made it politically untenable to name it "The Third National Bank of the United States." The name "Federal Reserve" was less politically charged but still sounded official. Note that all the national banks and the Federal Reserve were actually private banks with special contractual relationships with the federal government.

Secretary of the Treasury Alexander Hamilton initially pushed for a national bank in the United States in 1790 during the first George Washington administration. Hamilton argued that the fledgling new nation needed to have the United States Bank as an emergency measure to assure foreign nations and investors that the U.S. economy would be stable and have access to credit as it became established.

Hamilton asked Congress to establish the bank for just twenty years in order to carry out this emergency function, and he said that after twenty years the bank would no longer be needed. Jefferson and Madison disagreed with this plan, but Congress sided with Hamilton and authorized the bank.

The twenty-year plan worked as Hamilton recommended and did help establish the United States as a stable economy with access to needed credit.

However, many leaders felt that it was the Constitution—rather than the bank—that reassured creditors and created economic stability. Specifically, they pointed to Article I where the Constitution said: "All debts contracted and engagements entered into before the adoption of this Constitution shall be as valid against the United States under this Constitution as under the Articles of Confederation."

This came as a pleasant surprise to most creditors because the practice in Europe at the time was for nations in debt to simply reorganize themselves, adopt a new name, and refuse to pay the debts of the earlier government.

Institutions Sometimes Outlive Their Purpose

Whether the United States Bank actually helped the U.S. establish its credit and stability or not, when the charter ran out twenty years later, supporters didn't want it to dissolve. Once established, institutions are often strongly against their own demise, even if their original purpose has been fulfilled and become obsolete. As Ronald Reagan said, "The closest thing we will see to immortality is a government program."

> *Once established, institutions are often strongly against their own demise, even if their original purpose has been fulfilled and become obsolete.*

Jefferson and Madison argued that a national bank was a bad idea. But the promoters of keeping the national bank even after the twenty years had elapsed had the following major arguments in favor of keeping the bank:

- The Congress must oversee the coining of money, as outlined in the Constitution, so that the currency won't be like some foreign currencies where the people are cheated by the government or banks mixing lesser-value metals into the coinage.
- Metal money is difficult to manage, transport, carry around for large purchases, etc. Paper money is much easier to use.
- A central bank can carry out these functions better than Congress.

- Without a central bank, all private banks can just print their own currency, and citizens won't know which bank currencies are good and which won't be honored by the bank that issued them.

- Without a central bank currency, one bank won't honor the currency of other banks, so citizens won't know which currencies to use.

- All of this will greatly hurt the carrying out of business and thereby reduce the wealth of the nation.

- A private bank with a special contract with Congress can be required by contract to loan money to the government at low interest rates, and this may be needed in times of war or major economic challenge.

Indeed, it was this last point that Hamilton felt most justified the need for a national bank. During the Civil War, the same argument was made. In contrast, those against a national bank felt that a strong economy would be the best guarantee of the nation's ability to borrow. They also argued that in times of national duress, patriotic American bankers would give low-interest loans as needed. (In fact, history had already proven this to be true.)

As for the other arguments for a national bank, the truth is that many bank currencies in world history *had* cheated the people by mixing lesser metals into the coinage of precious metals. Some governments engaged in the same practices. Fourteenth-century writer Nicholas Oresme suggested that this debasement of the currency by the government may have been the major reason the Roman Empire fell.

Also, nearly all people prefer paper currency because of the difficulty of using metal in exchange, savings, transport, transfer, etc. And, in truth, leaving it up to private banks to determine their own rules for currency has caused many problems in history.

The Bank Solution

But Jefferson, Madison, and other critics of a national bank pointed out that all of these problems could be addressed without a national bank simply by requiring all currencies to be redeemable in gold or silver. Indeed, the framers anticipated this when they wrote in the original draft of the Constitution that the Congress would have the authority to "emit bills of credit." This was discussed and taken out because the framers were deeply concerned with governments and others debasing the currency.

> *Jefferson, Madison, and other critics of a national bank pointed out that all of these problems could be addressed without a national bank simply by requiring all currencies to be redeemable in gold or silver.*

In fact, the early Americans were so frustrated with the practice of governments and banks in the world mixing lesser metals into coinage and even more often cheating on paper currencies that one of the early laws passed by Congress was the Coinage Act in 1792.

In this law, those who cheated the people by debasing the currency were sentenced to the death penalty!

The founding generation saw such cheating simply as theft, and it considered this behavior especially heinous when governments did it. Generations later, economist John Maynard Keynes wrote: "Lenin was certainly right. There is no subtler, no surer means of overturning the existing basis of Society than to debauch the currency. The process engages all the hidden forces of economic law on the side of destruction, and does it in a manner which not one man in a million is able to diagnose."

Debauching the currency applies to both mixing inferior metals into coins and printing fiat currency, which inflates.

Four Types of Currency

Note that the phrase "bills of credit" used in the original draft of the Constitution means something specific. There are basically four kinds of currency. First, gold or silver has its own value and is considered sound currency because it can be exchanged for goods and services and also exchanged for its own value.

Second, bills of credit (also called "debt currency") consist of paper money that can be taken to any bank or to the government and exchanged directly for gold or silver. This is also seen as sound money, since it can be traded for goods and services or traded for precious metal that has its own value.

Third, debased money is a metal that cheats those who take it because it has been mixed with lesser metals or is paper money that cannot be traded for precious metals or that is traded for less precious metal than the paper money claims.

Fourth, fiat money is accepted by some in exchange for goods and services but cannot be traded for precious metals, gems, assets, or anything else with its own value. It is really only paper and ink.

Some people argue that fiat money is just as good as sound money as long as everyone accepts this currency in trade for goods and services. The problem is that not everyone *does* accept fiat money at the same value as sound money, as any who have travelled internationally and had to exchange their currency have discovered. Because of this, gold and silver tend to increase in value over time, while printed money tends to lose its value.

Others argue that gold and silver only increase in value when measured against fiat money, that metals are actually a constant store of value against which fiat currencies fluctuate. This is accurate, but when compared to buying power in land, goods, and services, gold and silver do tend to increase in value over time.

Economist Murray Rothbard used to laugh over this debate between steady versus increased value, since our modern currencies tend to lose value over time. At the end of a debate, Rothbard sometimes asked why we would want a steady economy when we could have one that increases our wealth naturally.

Aristocratic Money

When printed currency loses its value, it is called *inflation* (be-cause more money is needed to achieve the same value), and it has been a serious problem for many nations over time.

This is especially problematic in democratic nations because the wealthy classes who know better tend to transfer their fiat currency into gold, silver, gems, land, real estate, stock, and other things that are sound (meaning they can be traded for goods and services and that they also have value on their own). But people in the lower and middle classes often keep their savings in fiat money.

In the very worst of times, the rich get richer and the poor get poorer. When the economy shifts up and down, which happens periodically in any system, the wealthy are left with gold, silver, gems, and land (and the price of these tend to go up), while the middle and lower classes are left with worthless pieces of paper.

> *Fiat money benefits an aristocratic upper class and hurts the democratic tendencies of society. In contrast, sound money treats everyone equally by holding and often increasing in value regardless of economic ups and downs.*

In short, fiat money benefits an aristocratic upper class and hurts the democratic tendencies of society. In contrast, sound money treats everyone equally by holding and often increasing in value regardless of economic ups and downs.

The framers thought everyone's wealth should increase during difficult times (and the rest of the time), and so they emphasized the vital necessity of sound money.

The Fiat Problem

The framers were very familiar with the dangers of fiat money. As Orrin Woodward wrote in his book *RESOLVED: 13 Resolutions for LIFE*, "It's not well known, but outside of the medieval Chinese, colonial Massachusetts was the first government to issue fiat paper money [though various banks had done it in history]. Fiat money is money not backed by gold or any other valuable [commodity]." After detailing a failed Massachusetts state military conflict in Quebec in 1690, Woodward explained that the "...soldiers arrived back in Boston, ill-tempered and demanding payment of their salaries. The Massachusetts State government concluded that printing £7,000 of paper notes to pay the soldiers was safer than having soldiers unpaid within the city."

The government announced that it would make the notes redeemable for gold and silver at some point in the future, just "not now." It also promised to never issue fiat notes again. It later defaulted on both promises.

For example, just four months later, the Massachusetts government began printing more fiat currency. Predictably, this fiat currency inflated, meaning that it would only buy about 60 percent of what regular gold or silver currency could purchase. The government passed a law requiring everyone to accept the fiat money at the same rate as gold and silver. As a result, people kept their gold and silver hidden and spent only the fiat bills. The economy almost collapsed, and the British Crown eventually had to intervene, stop the printing presses, and restore monetary trust.

Later, the Continental Congress printed similar fiat money to finance the Revolutionary War. This led to a near-depressionary economy in the 1780s, which in fact was the major cause of sending delegates to meet in the Constitutional Convention in 1787 to try to fix the situation.

The framers, who had witnessed the dangers of fiat money firsthand, strongly pushed to give full faith and credit to all national debts and to give only Congress the right to coin money and to oversee all weights and measurements. They knew that these were actually national security issues because they had witnessed the negative effects of debased and fiat currency on the nation. They also removed the phrase "emit bills of credit" from the original draft of the Constitution. They wanted sound metal money, pure and simple. And they wanted to protect the nation from inflation.

> *They removed the phrase "emit bills of credit" from the original draft of the Constitution. They wanted sound metal money, pure and simple.*

In *Gold: The Once and Future Money*, historian Nathan Lewis notes that:

> Continuous inflationary periods are often accompanied by a conspicuous decline of morality and civility....Histori-

ans recount that civilizations fell into decadence as people lived for immediate gratification rather than saving and investing—and financial deterioration led to deterioration in the personal relationships....

It's no coincidence that the Golden Ages of Rome, Britain, and the United States were also eras where the currencies themselves were as good as gold.

Classical economist David Ricardo wrote in *Principles of Political Economy and Taxation*: "Experience...shows that neither a state nor a bank ever had the unrestricted power of issuing paper money without abusing that power; in all states, therefore, the issue of paper money ought to be under some check and control; and none seems so proper for that purpose as that of subjecting the issuers of paper money to the obligation of paying their notes either in gold coin or bullion."

Unfortunately in our modern world, the voices against fiat money, national banks like the Fed, the income tax, and the Seventeenth Amendment are often angry and extreme—causing the majority of Americans to tune out their strident criticism. But a national bank and fiat money have serious drawbacks, as the framers knew.

Fiat Money Leads to Inflation

Jefferson and Madison were able to convince America to get rid of the First Bank of the United States in 1811, mainly because it had created an era of massive inflation in the 1790s. President Jefferson also paid off the national debt, balanced the budget, and reduced both spending and taxes.

Unfortunately, Congress chartered the Second National Bank in 1816. Andrew Jackson later helped get rid of the Second National Bank, balance the budget, and pay off the national debt as Jefferson and Madison had worked to accomplish earlier.

This battle between limited government, balanced budgets, and economic frugality on the one hand versus big government, printing more money, using inflationary debt to pay for government programs, and constantly increasing government spending on the other hand has raged throughout America's history. Each time that the frugal philosophy has won for a while, it has been followed by a return to big spending.

For example, Jackson's hard-fought victories in paying off the national debt and getting rid of the Second National Bank were followed by an era of little regulation on currency. The plan of the framers was for Congress to coin all currency and for any bank currencies to be regulated so they could only be sound money—never debased or fiat. Unfortunately, U.S. leaders argued about whether to have a national bank but did little to stop the widespread use of debased and fiat bank currencies across the nation.

Historian W. Cleon Skousen wrote:

> ...by the time of the Civil War there were thousands of banks issuing thousands of different kinds of bank notes. Furthermore, many banks were issuing far more notes than

they had reserves [so that not everyone could trade in their paper currency for gold or silver]. There was also a tremendous amount of counterfeiting. Before long, the whole system began to falter.

When the Civil War required vast new expenditures... Congress felt compelled to issue fiat money. These "greenbacks" could not be redeemed in gold or silver and were limited somewhat in the things for which they could be spent. Their value soon dropped to around 35 cents.

Finally, in 1878, Congress promised to redeem the greenbacks in gold. This changed the greenbacks from cheap fiat money to debt money [or bills of credit], redeemable at face value. At first, there was a run on gold as people traded in their greenbacks, but when they found they really could get gold, then people didn't want it. They returned their gold to the bank and took back paper money instead. This left the United States on the gold standard until 1933.

Repeated Mistakes

In 1913, the Federal Reserve became, in effect, a new national bank of the United States. It printed bills of credit, redeemable in gold or silver, until 1933. Unfortunately, the Fed has

> *In 1913, the Federal Reserve became, in effect, a new national bank of the United States.*

printed fiat money ever since. Over time, this has helped increase the gap between the very wealthy and the middle and lower classes in the United States.

Those promoting the Federal Reserve made the same arguments—outlined above—as proponents of the First and Second National Banks. And the same criticisms of a national bank or Federal Reserve still apply. The real solution is sound money—which would help increase the wealth of all Americans over time.

Nevertheless, President Wilson's push for a bigger government required the ability of the government to more easily borrow larger amounts and to print money at will, and that was the argument that won the day when Congress authorized the Federal Reserve.

The impact of that move has been huge and lasting. To summarize: The Sixteenth Amendment allowed Congress to get more money directly from the people without the consent of the states. The Seventeenth Amendment removed the naturally frugal tendency of the Senate and led to increased demand in Congress for additional spending programs. And finally, the creation of the Fed gave Congress a more efficient mechanism to borrow, print, and spend greater amounts of money as it deemed desirable.

Consequences of the Turning Point

Together, these three 1913 events caused an increased desire in Washington to spend, eliminated roadblocks to massive spending, and created easier mechanisms for taxing, borrowing, and printing money.

In short, 1913 was a banner year for big government. Only one more major thing was needed to open the floodgates of massive government. It would take years for it to come to fruition, but after Wilson's speech, it was only a matter of time.

Yes, the year was 1913. Philadelphia won the World Series over New York, and the first recorded pie-in-the-face scene showed up in cinema. Cracker Jack began adding a prize to each package, and Buffalo Bill Cody shut down his famous Wild West Show. The old was out, and a new era was in.

For example, J.P. Morgan died in 1913, and Richard Nixon was born. Cy Young had just retired, and Vince Lombardi was born. Harriet Tubman died, and Rosa Parks was born. The Fiftieth Anniversary celebration of Gettysburg was held, and the song "Danny Boy" was released.

The year was 1913, and things were about to change in big ways. The modern zipper became popular that year, and stainless steel was invented. Ford Motor Company used the first moving assembly line in history in 1913, and the first crossword puzzle was published in *The New York World*.

Yet few noticed that the Turning Point away from American freedom had come in a short speech followed by three world-shifting events. The Jeffersonian style of limited government ended this year, and a new era of big government was born. It was just one year…but what a year.

A few years later, things would change even more.

CHAPTER 5

World-Shifting Event #4: *United States v. Butler* in 1936

"The pen is mightier than the sword."
—Edward Bulwer-Lytton

The workings of the court in the United States often read like a "secret" history of America. This is not surprising, given that the people are closely involved in electing presidents, senators, congressmen, governors, and state legislators but have little direct say about the Supreme Court.

The "Secret" History

Most Americans have heard of a few major cases, such as the *Dred Scott* decision (allowing slavery) or *Roe v. Wade* (allowing abortions). But for many Americans, the processes and actions of the court seem distant and technical. The truth is that court decisions have had a great impact on the freedom and prosperity of the American people. In fact, in 1936 an obscure case called the *United States v. Butler* became the fourth great event in the Turning Point of Freedom that began in 1913.

But before we delve into the *Butler* case, understand that it wasn't the first major case that changed American history. The court has a long tradition of major decisions that have drastically impacted American freedom and prosperity.

A Brief History of Critical Supreme Court Cases

For example, as early as 1803, the court began to assert its own authority over the other branches of government. This occurred in the case *Marbury v. Madison,* as Chief Justice John Marshall announced in his opinion that "the Supreme Court was the exclusive and final arbiter of what was constitutional and what was not, and furthermore, that its decisions were binding on all branches of government."

This was a significant change to the original Constitution, which gave the court the final say in determining the winner and the loser in any given case but said nothing about the power to use a case as decisive precedent for any other case—and certainly granted the judiciary no power over any *other* branch of government.

For many decades, law students have been taught differently, and the legal profession has mostly accepted that setting precedent is part of the court's role. But it wasn't originally so. Again, as mentioned, the original intent of the founding was for the court to have the final say in any given case, but not beyond.

Before *Marbury v. Madison,* the Congress had the right to read the Constitution and interpret it for itself, as did the president. Each of the three branches, and also the states, were intended to be independent and to apply their own interpretation of the Constitution within their constitutional powers.

Thomas Jefferson wrote to Abigail Adams: "You seem to think it devolved on the judges to decide on the validity of the sedition law, but nothing in the Constitution has given them the right to decide for the executive, more than to the executive to decide for them. Both [the Supreme Court and the president] are equally independent in the sphere of action assigned to them."

He also wrote: "My construction of the Constitution...is that each department is truly dependent of the others, and has an equal right to decide for itself what is the meaning of the Constitution in the cases submitted to its action..."

Jefferson wrote the following specifically about the decision in *Marbury v. Madison*: "The Constitution intended that the three great branches of the government should be...independent of each other...It did not intend to give the judiciary control over the executive...I have long wished for a proper occasion to have the gratuitous opinion of *Marbury v. Madison* brought before the public, and denounced as not law."

Long before the *Butler* case of 1936, Thomas Jefferson foresaw the problem created by *Marbury v. Madison*. He wrote:

It has long, however, been my opinion, and I have never shrunk from its expression...that the germ of dissolution of our federal government is in the constitution of the federal judiciary; an irresponsible body... working like gravity by night and by day, gaining a little today and a little tomorrow, and advancing its noiseless step like a thief...until all shall be usurped from the States, and the government of all be consolidated into one.

To this I am opposed; because when all government...in little as in great things, shall be drawn to Washington as the centre of all power, it will render powerless the checks provided of one government on another, and will become as venal and oppressive as the government from which we separated.

> *"To this I am opposed; because when all government...in little as in great things, shall be drawn to Washington as the centre of all power, it will render powerless the checks provided of one government on another, and will become as venal and oppressive as the government from which we separated."*

Today much is made of the need for an independent judiciary, and in fact this was an important part of the constitutional system— the framers disliked the way British courts were subordinate to the Monarchy and Parliament. But the framers also wanted the executive and legislative branches to be independent of the judiciary. They also expected the state branches of government to be independent. Thus, Jefferson was deeply concerned about the *Marbury* decision.

Two Other Pivotal Cases

Nor were Jefferson's concerns far-fetched. In 1816, the court ruled in *Martin v. Hunter Lessee* that the U.S. Supreme Court's rulings were above the decisions of the state supreme courts. The court also decided in this case that the Supreme Court was in charge of interpreting all federal law. Again, these two changes were not the original understanding of the framers of the United States Constitution.

In 1819, the court further decided (in the case *McCulloch v. Maryland*) that the federal government gets its power directly from the people, not through the states, and that the court also gets it power directly from the people rather than from the states or the Constitution. Thus, the court doesn't have to follow the Constitution word-for-word, but rather gets to determine for itself what "following it" actually means.

Note that under this interpretation, the court doesn't allow any other branch of government the same luxury. In other words, according to the court's decision in this case, the court gets to decide what its own powers are, regardless of what the Constitution or anyone else says on the subject, and it also gets to decide the powers of the other branches of government. Again, this is in direct contrast to the original intent of the framers.

As a result of these three cases, the court basically determined that it is above the other branches and levels of government because the Constitution means *whatever the court says it means.*

The court simply decided that it had more power and granted itself these increased powers not listed in the Constitution. This is clearly contrary to the intention of those who wrote and ratified the Constitution. Moreover, it has reduced the freedom and prosperity of the American people without ever being subject to an election, recall, or public debate.

> The court simply decided that it had more power and granted itself these increased powers not listed in the Constitution.

The technocracy within the judiciary has simply made these changes, and dozens of others, without asking for permission from the American people. It has claimed these powers based on the Constitution—though the document grants none of these powers. Building on this historical precedent, the court made another world-altering decision in 1936. Actually, it wasn't the decision that mattered in this case, but rather the written opinion of one court member.

The *Butler* Case

In 1936, two major trends collided: the three turning-point events of 1913 (passage of the Sixteenth and Seventeenth Amendments and the establishment of the Federal Reserve) and the continued expansion of the power of the court after the *Marbury v. Mad-*

ison case. This all came together in the case known as the *United States v. Butler*.

As it happens, President Franklin D. Roosevelt agreed with Wilson's push for a much bigger government, and in fact felt that the government needed to be significantly larger than even Wilson suggested. FDR even attempted to increase the size of the Supreme Court so he could fill the court with justices who would support his many attempts to expand the size and role of the federal government.

Before 1913, the federal government could not directly tax the income of the populace. Any proposed federal spending had to be approved by both the representatives of the people (House) and of the states (Senate), and the government had no mechanism for printing money at will. All of these changed, as discussed in earlier chapters, during the Turning Point of Freedom in 1913.

But even after 1913, the federal government was constitutionally limited in how much it could spend. It could, after 1913, increase taxes and debt and print money at will. But it still could not spend money on any program that wasn't allowed under the Constitution.

This changed after the *Butler* case. While the *Butler* case never received the publicity of cases such as *Dred Scott* or *Roe v. Wade*, it nevertheless had a drastic and lasting impact on American society. And while the case was actually about agricultural policy, which has long since ceased to be directly relevant to modern society, a few small details of the court opinion in the case are still guiding our entire political model.

Specifically, before the *Butler* case, the federal government was limited to spending money only on the things explicitly outlined in the Constitution (the twenty powers enumerated in Article I, Section 8, and as listed in Chapter 2) and other things necessary for the "general welfare" of the nation. In the founding era, the phrase "general welfare" referred to things which benefitted *every* citizen in the nation—as opposed to private and special welfare, which only benefit specific people or groups.

> *Before the* Butler *case, the federal government was limited to spending money only on the things explicitly outlined in the Constitution.*

For example, James Madison wrote in *Federalist Paper* 41 that the General Welfare Clause did not allow Congress to do anything beyond the twenty powers listed in Article I, Section 8.

Not All Change Is Progress

As constitutional expert W. Cleon Skousen wrote:

The Founders looked upon the lawmaking process as a sacred trust. They therefore set up the most elaborate screening procedures ever devised by man. Although more than 20,000 bills and resolutions are introduced in Congress each session, only about 10 percent survive the screening process.

Originally, Congress was supposed to pass bills and spend money only for the GENERAL welfare of the whole country. Gradually, the chains of the Constitution have eroded so that today there are numerous bills for PRIVATE welfare. Consequently, there are two kinds of bills introduced in Congress: (1) public bills which apply to the whole nation, and (2) private bills which apply to individual citizens or groups of people.

Before the *Butler* case, all federal spending was required to benefit the whole nation equally. After the case, the government could spend money on anything it thought would be "good" for the nation.

> *Before the* **Butler** *case, all federal spending was required to benefit the whole nation equally. After the case, the government could spend money on anything it thought would be "good" for the nation.*

As summarized by *The Oxford Companion to the Supreme Court of the United States*: "Justice Owen J. Roberts' opinion for the majority... did...settle a long-standing dispute concerning the taxing power of Congress. Article I, Section 8, authorizes Congress to levy taxes 'to pay the debts and provide for the common defense and general welfare of the United States...' James Madison contended that 'general welfare' purposes were limited to authorizations elsewhere in the Constitution...."

However, the court's official decision in *Butler* boldly declared that "...the power of Congress to authorize expenditure of public moneys for public purposes is not limited by the direct grants of legislative power found in the Constitution." In other words, *Congress can do anything it wants—even if it is not "constitutional"—as* long the court upholds it. Indeed, if the court calls it "constitutional," it

is, regardless of what the actual document says.

> *Congress can do anything it wants—even if it is not "constitutional"—as long the court upholds it. Indeed, if the court calls it "constitutional," it is, regardless of what the actual document says.*

A Tortured Construction

This is a major shift away from American constitutional freedom, and some of the justices realized this. According to the *Oxford Companion*, "Justices Harlan F. Stone, Louis D. Brandeis, and Benjamin Cardazo dissented. In a scathing rebuttal, Stone called Roberts' ruling 'a tortured construction of the Constitution.' But the most widely noted language in Stone's dissent was his warning against judicial arrogance: 'Courts are not the only agency of government that must be assumed to have the capacity to govern...The only check upon our own exercise of power is our own sense of self-restraint.'"

> *Butler set the precedent for the court allowing congressional taxation and expenditures far beyond the twenty powers listed in the original Constitution.*

But this view lost, and *Butler* set the precedent for the court allowing congressional taxation and expenditures far beyond the twenty powers listed in the original Constitution. "In retrospect," the *Oxford Companion* continues, "the principal positive contribution of the *Butler* majority is the principle, as restated by Chief Justice Warren E. Burger in *Fullilove v. Klutznick* (1980), that the power to provide for the general welfare 'is an independent grant of legislative authority, distinct from other broad congressional powers.'"

In other words: This decision gave the federal government a new power, granted by the court, allowing for laws about spending to be upheld that couldn't have passed muster before.

The result of the *Butler* decision has been a Congress that has defined general welfare as anything the Congress thought would benefit the nation, even if it wasn't authorized by the Constitution—and a court that has supported this interpretation. Through this case, a major check on the federal government was wiped out, though few Americans at the time took any notice.

Justice Sandra Day O'Connor pointed out in 1987 that since the *Butler* decision in 1936, the court *has never once struck down any act of Congress as beyond the authority granted by the Constitution.* The explosion of spending which followed *Butler* and the new

> *Since the* **Butler** *decision in 1936, the court has never once struck down any act of Congress as beyond the authority granted by the Constitution.*

American view of the Constitution as widely supportive of whatever Congress passes has drastically reshaped the United States. We've shifted from a Jefferson-style limited government focused on free enterprise to a massive bureaucracy that continues to regulate all aspects of the economy and gets bigger with each passing year.

Jefferson's Warning

The dissenting justices in 1936 wrote that the *Butler* case showed a judicial arrogance and warned, as noted earlier, "The only check upon our own exercise of power is our own sense of self-restraint." Jefferson had argued the same point over a century earlier.

Concerned with the fact that all branches of government except the Supreme Court could be checked by others, and with the fact that the Supreme Court had shown in *Marbury v. Madison* that it considered itself above the other branches of government, Jefferson argued for an amendment that would effectively check the court.

Jefferson wrote:

There was another amendment of which none of us thought at the time [of ratification of the Constitution], and in the omission of which lurks the germ that is to destroy this happy combination of national powers in the general government for matters of national concern, and independent powers in the states for what concerns the states severally....

I deem it indispensable to the continuance of this government that they [the opinions of the Supreme Court] should be submitted to some practical and impartial control; and this, to be impartial, must be compounded of a mixture of state and federal authorities... I do not charge the judges with willful and ill-intentioned error; but honest error must be arrested where its toleration leads to public ruin.

Such an amendment was never adopted, and the court continued to expand its power and that of the government leading up to the *Butler* case and even more after the *Butler* decision.

The Aftermath of the *Butler* Case

The results have been disastrous for American freedom, free enterprise, and opportunity. Since 1936, twelve of the thirteen U.S. presidents have drastically increased U.S. spending over the levels of their predecessors (only President Truman presided over significantly reduced spending, and that was only due to the end of the war; even he tried to increase many spending programs).

In comparison, of the thirteen presidents leading up to 1936, only four significantly increased U.S. per capita budgetary spending. Two held spending levels basically the same as their predecessors, and seven of the thirteen presidents reduced spending compared to the president they replaced.

In the post-*Butler* system, in order to meet the desired federal spending, taxes are raised, and debts, deficits, and government spending balloon. When these traditional sources of money fail, the government simply prints more money through the Federal Reserve. This inflates our fiat currency, distorts the natural ups and downs of the business cycle and recessions, and increases the divide between the wealthy (who store their wealth in non-fiat assets) and the middle and lower classes.

Clearly, the systemic change caused by the redefining of "general

welfare" in *United States v. Butler* created lasting structural alterations to how the United States government does its business. Indeed,
after the *Butler* case, "the federal budget jumped from six billion to
six *hundred* billion in one generation." It has consistently increased
ever since.

Moreover, it is doubtful that this trend will be reversed without a
major economic depression and a significant change to the system
created by the three changes in 1913 and the *Butler* case of 1936.

> *These seemingly
> small events changed
> the entire American
> culture by permanently
> altering the relationship
> between the people,
> the government,
> and the economy.*

These seemingly small events
changed the entire American culture
by permanently altering the relation-
ship between the people, the government, and the economy. Only a small
percentage of the American people
took part in these four changes, but
their influence remains today. In fact,
regardless of which party wins major
state and national elections, these four changes drive federal spending increasingly up.

The good news: These events demonstrate that a few small
changes led by a few knowing and committed people can have a
drastic impact on the future. Such changes can be positive, not just
negative like those of 1913/1936. We have reached the point where
such positive changes and current turning-point events in the direction of freedom are needed.

CHAPTER 6

The Founding of Freedom in Modern Times

"There is no surer road to destruction
than prosperity without character."
—Calvin Coolidge

The United States Constitution provided the framework for the freest nation in all of history. Freedom incentivizes great things from people, and the Constitution released the potential of the American people and all those who would eventually call America their home.

The American founding generation was certainly not made up of perfect people, and the system the framers created had some glaring flaws. Still, the American founders understood freedom—political, spiritual, and financial—and they started the ball rolling in the right direction for freedom. We have so much to learn from them.

Let's start by understanding three vital lessons from the American founding. Each lesson on its own needs to be applied to our current world, and by applying all three, we will take a huge step toward restoring many freedoms which have been lost in the last century.

Lesson #1: A Wise Citizenry

The first lesson of the American founding is that the whole citizenry must understand freedom, or it is unlikely to last. The ancient Israelites and Anglo-Saxons required their youth to memorize the laws and governmental principles of the nation and pass them off in oral questioning to the town elders in order to become adults. They felt that unless the people knew the laws, freedom would certainly decrease.

Without a wise populace that understands how freedom works and takes an active part in maintaining it, no free society has ever lasted. Indeed, free societies tend to break down as soon as a rising generation, basking in its peace and prosperity, forgets how vitally important freedom is and how quickly it can be lost.

The loss of freedom usually occurs when the people elect leaders but then stop taking part in societal governance on a daily basis. When the protection of freedom is left to a few officials, it is always lost. Only the close care and participation of the people in what happens in their government can keep freedom alive.

John Adams wrote in 1765: "A native of America who cannot read or write is as rare…as a comet or an earthquake. It has been observed that we are all of us lawyers, divines, politicians, and philosophers." Modern readers tend to read this differently than those who read it in Adams' day. We think Adams is saying that most Americans are educated and some of us are lawyers, some are priests, some are politicians, and some are philosophers.

But Adams was actually saying that nearly every American has the education of a lawyer and *also* the learning of a priest, politician, and philosopher combined. Adams' point was that the average American education combines the wisdom and knowledge of *all* these fields of learning.

Adams continued in this same quote: "And I have good authorities to say that all candid foreigners who have passed through this country and conversed freely with all sorts of people here will allow that they have never seen so much knowledge and civility among the common people in any part of the world....Liberty cannot be preserved without a general knowledge among the people."

> *"Liberty cannot be preserved without a general knowledge among the people."*

Alexis de Tocqueville wrote: "In New England every citizen receives the elementary notions of human knowledge; he is taught, moreover, the doctrines and evidences of his religion, the history of his country, and the leading features of its Constitution. In the states of Connecticut and Massachusetts, it is extremely rare to find a man imperfectly acquainted with all these things, and a person wholly ignorant of them is a sort of phenomenon."

Constitutional scholar W. Cleon Skousen summed it up: "In the American colonies the intention was to have all children **taught**

the fundamentals of reading, writing, and arithmetic, **so that they could go on to become well-informed citizens** through their own diligent self-study."

The Knowledge of Free People

Some modern readers may argue that this is the same system we use today. The reality, however, is that in the founding generations, the average adult read much more deeply than most moderns. Those who doubt this should note that the *Federalist Papers*—which challenge the average law student today—were written as simple newspaper articles for typical farmers and merchants in 1789 New York.

As intricate, deep, and detailed as the *Federalist Papers* are, it is clear that the typical political education of the citizen in 1789 America was much more advanced than that of most Americans in our time. A simple reading of letters among the people of this time shows the same thing.

> *The typical political education of the citizen in 1789 America was much more advanced than that of most Americans in our time.*

Free people are exactly that: a free people, not just a mass of uneducated people led by a few aristocratic and highly-educated leaders at the top. If the broad masses of people don't have the same level of understanding and learning as their governors, judges, and presidents, they simply will not maintain their freedoms.

The same is true even if the masses are highly trained in professional careers but still generally less educated on political and economic principles than their representatives and other leaders. Allan Bloom pointed out in *The Closing of the American Mind* that the last powerful nation to be as highly trained but broadly uneducated as the modern U.S. was Hitler's Germany in the 1930s and 1940s.

In short, freedom exists when the masses of people are deeply read in the ideas and principles of freedom. When the people stop reading and considering the concepts of political and economic freedom in a consistent way, they always lose their freedoms.

> *The last powerful nation to be as highly trained but broadly uneducated as the modern U.S. was Hitler's Germany in the 1930s and 1940s.*

Lesson # 2: Created Equal

A second lesson is that all men and women are created equal. The founders got this right in the *Declaration of Independence,* but failed to apply this true principle to all men and women. The deep flaw of slavery was later corrected in the Civil War, but the cost to the nation was huge and incredibly painful.

Other inequalities lasted even longer and took much pain and struggle to overcome. All people are created equal, and freedom can only be built on this common understanding.

Freedom for a few, while the rest of

> *Freedom for a few, while the rest of the people are denied freedoms, isn't freedom at all.*

the people are denied freedoms, isn't freedom at all. Where political freedom is concerned, inalienable rights and freedoms must be applied to everyone equally. This is the main purpose of government, and when it falls short of this (or tries to do much beyond protecting equal rights), freedom for all is decreased. History is absolutely clear on this point.

Whenever the majority accepts the reduction of freedom for a few people—for whatever reason—it always comes back to bite them. When freedom is abridged for a few, it is reduced for everyone. There is no exception to this principle.

And when one kind of freedom—political, spiritual, or financial—is decreased, all freedom is lessened. Likewise, when any one type of freedom is increased, all freedom benefits—for everyone.

Thus, each and every citizen of a free nation—or one that wants to be free—should spend a lot of time and effort studying and promoting freedom. Unless a free nation is made up of a people in love with freedom and dedicated to it, liberty will be lost. If the regular people leave freedom and governance to the experts, freedom is lost—always.

Of course, the founders knew that people are different and that no two people are precisely equal in anything. But they also understood that the only way to maintain freedom is for the government and law to treat all people equally under the law.

Lesson # 3: Auxiliary Precautions

A third lesson of the founding is that it is the nature of power to centralize and then expand. Nearly every person or entity with power is impacted by this reality.

Therefore, when the people establish a government (or support one already established), they must divide its power into various entities that are forced to compete (balance) and keep each other in check. This is what the framers established by separating the federal government into three distinct branches and providing constitutional balances between each branch.

They also set up the new American nation with local, state, and federal levels of government and built in checks and balances between each level. And above all these levels and branches, they knew the people would need to be the ultimate overseers of government.

The framers called this model of separating powers into competing entities that check and balance each other by an interesting name: "auxiliary precautions." Engineers are taught the importance of primary systems and auxiliaries that kick in if the primary systems fail. In political science, the same principles are vital.

For example, the primary method of powering most homes and buildings in developed nations is the electric grid. Electricity flows through the wires into the building and provides the power for lights, computers, heaters, etc. But when the power goes out, some homes and buildings have an auxiliary.

Those who don't have any auxiliary power must wait for the

power to return through the normal means. Homes and buildings with an auxiliary, however, are able to generate power without interruption until the primary power begins to flow again.

The Head of Free Governments

In the case of government, the American founders saw the people as the primary leaders of the nation. The people held the power, some of which they delegated to government for certain functions like national security and law enforcement. The rest of the power, as described in the Ninth and Tenth Amendments, was reserved to the states or the people themselves.

As long as the people performed their role as leaders of the nation, the framers argued, America would remain free. And because the nation would be free, the citizens would be able to seek and obtain prosperity, happiness, family success, and whatever else they desired.

The people were likely to do this, the framers said, as long as they were moral and virtuous, widely read and well educated in the principles of government and economics and all the arts and sciences, willing to voluntarily sacrifice for the good of the nation, quick to voluntarily help others in need (not primarily through government channels), and actively involved in the daily actions of government. If such citizens led the nation, freedom would not be lost.

But if a time ever came where the people forgot the importance of freedom or stopped doing their job of making sure the society remained free, the nation remained secure, and criminals were unable to take away the hard-earned life and assets of the people, then the auxiliary precautions would kick in. The framers knew that this was vital. The great value of auxiliary precautions is discussed in *Federalist* 51 and 63.

These auxiliary precautions, as mentioned in the *Federalist Papers*, included the following:

1. A written Constitution, so the people can see exactly what the government is allowed to do
2. A constitutional provision that the government cannot do anything not explicitly allowed in the Constitution
3. The separation of powers between local, state, and federal governments and also between the legislative, executive, and judicial branches of government
4. Checks and balances between all of these levels and branches
5. A limit of twenty powers for the federal government, spelled out in detail in Article I, Section 8 of the Constitution
6. Periodic elections to allow the people to remove officials as needed

There are several other auxiliary precautions listed in the Constitution and discussed in the *Federalist Papers*, but these are the main ones.

As long as the people do their part to keep the government in check, the framers taught, America will remain free. If the people shirk their duties, these auxiliary precautions will hopefully slow down the loss of freedom long enough for the people to notice and take proper action to keep their freedoms.

This is exactly what has occurred. Unfortunately, the people stopped fully leading many decades ago, and today even the auxiliary precautions are beginning to wear thin.

It is time for Americans to once again take a stand for freedom. Hopefully, they will do this before it is too late.

The future of freedom and prosperity depends on how well we make this needed change. The three lessons covered in this chapter are only a few of the many things we can learn from the American founders and other leaders of freedom through history.

In fact, one great needed change in modern nations is for the citizens to do a lot more reading and thinking about history and the principles of freedom. The future of freedom literally depends on citizens doing such reading. These three lessons are vital, and though we could certainly cover many more, these are enough to get us started.

Seven Human Interactions

The economist Murray Rothbard noted that there are basically only seven major ways people interact with each other:

1. Charity/gifts/service
2. Voluntary exchange

3. Assault

4. Robbery

5. Slavery

6. Murder

7. War

Of course, the ideal is for nearly all human relations to focus on the first two, and government was originally established to help stop the other five negative types of interactions.

But in order for government to effectively fight these negatives, it must have enough power to do so, and with such power comes the danger, as Lord Acton warned, of abusing that power. In short, government is necessary to help stop assault, robbery, slavery, murder, and war—but it can also use its power to engage in these things. Through history, in fact, more governments have abused power than have not.

When this happens, when government power is turned from protecting against these five things (assault, robbery, slavery, murder, and war) to allowing or even causing these things, freedom and prosperity are lessened.

The American founding generation established the U.S. Constitution with these principles in mind. They wanted government to protect against these kinds of negatives and to protect the rights of free exchange and voluntary charity. Knowing that power often corrupts, they set the Constitution up to keep any one person or agency from getting too much power.

But they knew that the whole system would depend on citizens who kept an eye on government and kept it in line. Without such citizens, no nation stays free.

Today, we simply must return America to the focus on freedom and prosperity that made it the world's greatest free leader in history. We must get back to being the kind of citizens the framers envisioned. We must clarify what is wrong with our current system, take stock of what is broken, and then take action.

So what can *you* do about it? Will you be one of the few who restore freedom?

CHAPTER 7

Wanted: A Small Group of Committed Citizens

"There are two primary choices in life: to accept conditions as they exist, or accept the responsibility for changing them."
—Dennis Waitley

The problems I've detailed may seem overwhelming. You may feel powerless. But understand that fixing them doesn't require *every* American citizen—just a small but committed few.

Only a few people got on the *Mayflower*, but this event changed the world forever. Only a few sailed with Columbus, or even knew of his journey. Only a few stood firmly for their religion while the Roman soldiers herded them into the arenas to be slain by lions. Only a few participated—both for and against—in the life, trial, and crucifixion of Jesus Christ.

Only a few took part in the Glorious Revolution or the Thirty Years War. Only a few helped ratify the Magna Carta. Only a few supported Gautama Buddha in his drive for a better world or Gandhi in his similar campaign many centuries later.

Only a few stood firm against the British in the Revolutionary War, and only a few went to war to stop Hitler. Only a few brought us freedom through the U.S. Constitution, and only a few fought to spread those rights to all people. Only a few took action to promote civil rights for all, and only a few led the 1913 and 1936 events which created a Turning Point away from freedom.

In the coming Turning Point just ahead, a significant few will make all the difference in what direction our society takes. Moreover, this relatively few who will make the difference for literally billions in the next generations are alive today—though most have no idea that this is ahead for them.

None of us know exactly what the issues or events will be that sway the direction of the future. But history shows us undeniably that such a Turning Point will come. It also shows us what kind of people typically lead such events, and what is necessary to be one of the few that chooses the direction of the future.

What Will You Do with Your "Dash"?

Many important thinkers have proclaimed the power of the few and taught how a few people in history or business or society usually sway the reality for everyone else.

For example, one excellent book on this topic is appropriately entitled *The Vital Few* by Jonathan Hughes.

Orrin Woodward has spoken extensively about "the 5 percent versus the 95 percent," the few versus the masses. Where most people are willing to be satisfied with a basic level of happiness and success, the few will accept nothing but greatness. We need more who are willing to be the few.

Best-selling author Chris Brady has also spoken about this numerous times, quoting the poem "The Dash" by Linda Ellis. As the poem says, most tombstones list the name of the deceased along with a birth date and a year of death. Everything between these two dates is summed up with a dash. What a way to describe your life!

Brady notes that all of us should want our lives to mean more than a simple dash. While most people may be content with the dash, a few strive to live their lives in ways that their dash truly means something great in the world—not to impress or boast, but to truly care, greatly serve, and genuinely improve the world.

I wrote of the few in my book *FreedomShift:*

Why are we losing our freedoms? Santayana warns that a people that forgets is destined to repeat history. We have forgotten the great stories of how our freedom was won and the principles that they teach....

Margaret Mead has been oft-quoted: 'Never doubt that a small group of thoughtful, committed citizens can change the world. In-

"Never doubt that a small group of thoughtful, committed citizens can change the world. Indeed, it is the only thing that ever has."

deed, it is the only thing that ever has.'

Sometimes a few small and simple things sway everything, like the straw that breaks the camel's back. Malcolm Gladwell called this a Tipping Point, and in science it is called Disparate Distribution. In 1800 economist J.B. Say coined the term *entrepreneur* to describe those who drive the economy, and defined it with Say's Law: 'Entrepreneurs are the significant minority who takes resources from unproductive places and make them productive.'

History calls it 'The Law of the Vital Few'; in math it is reflected in Factor Sparsity. In economics, the idea that small things guide the big things is often referred to as the 80-20 Rule or Pareto's Law. This concept asserts that 20 percent of our actions create 80 percent of the results and 20 percent of the people have 80 percent of the impact...Three percent of the population controls 97 percent of the wealth....

Three to five percent of the people make all the difference in major world Turning Points.

As we have seen, such Turning Points bring drastic changes to society, and yet they are usually led by a few committed people rather than a mass of society.

Three things are needed to ensure that freedom and widespread prosperity are increased in the decades ahead. Those who do these three things in their lives will qualify themselves—knowingly or unwittingly—to have influence and lead in the Turning

Point just ahead. As we have seen, such Turning Points bring drastic changes to society, and yet they are usually led by a few committed people rather than a mass of society. Indeed, the masses are nearly always focused on other things while the key events take place that change history.

So, what are the three things which qualify a person to be part of the few who will lead the coming Turning Point and hopefully sway it toward freedom?

CHAPTER 8

Solution #1:
Entrepreneurship

No matter how bad things get, the entrepreneurial spirit always stands up, fights back, and optimistically seeks to overcome all challenges.

Ken Kurson wrote in the September 2010 issue of *Esquire* that while the brutal economic conditions of the Great Recession should have been disheartening to most entrepreneurs, many of them have used the most difficult economic downturns and crises as opportunities for growth. Futurist Alvin Toffler predicted in his book *The Third Wave*, "There are powerful reasons for long-range optimism, even if the transitional years immediately ahead are likely to be stormy and crisis ridden."

The Entrepreneurial Spirit

America has overcome numerous national challenges since its inception. This is mostly because of the unconquerable enterprising spirit of its people and the way free government has unleashed human initiative, ingenuity, innovation, resiliency, tenacity, virtue, and drive.

But if the turning-point events of our day continue in the direction of force and away from freedom and economic opportunity, the values of free enterprise and political, economic, and spiritual freedom will decline to a point that extinguishes the American Dream.

This may seem like a far-fetched possibility. But the loss of freedom and financial opportunity since 1913 has been widespread and significant, and the loss of even half that amount in the decades ahead would end the American model for good. The loss of freedom just since 2000 is surprising, and the trend seems to be increasing.

In short, another Turning Point is needed, this time in the direction of more freedom and prosperity. And as with other such changes in history, a few key events led by a few key people will cause the coming Turning Point.

Entrepreneurship Rooted in National Character

Those who will make the big choices of the future will be proven leaders. Some will come from all arenas of life, from media and academia to military, government, and entertainment. But most will be successful entrepreneurs. The reason for this is that America, and in fact Western Civilization, was founded on the basis of commercialism.

During the American founding era, thought leaders debated

about what kind of character would be best for the new American nation. There are three major choices for a nation's central character: martial, religious, and commercial.

Note that each of these has a drastic impact on any society. For example, a martial nation is interested almost solely in war. This determines how children are raised (to be warriors), how the government is formatted (almost always a monarchy), and nearly every other major detail of how the society is structured.

Martial nations like ancient Sparta or Rome, and more recently the Soviet Union or Maoist China, are aggressive, unstable, and internally violent. Also, martial societies are always class societies, where the labor of the masses pays for the martial life of a small and ultra-wealthy upper class. Understandably, the American framers didn't want the United States to be a nation of peasants, aristocrats, and royals.

Societies with a religious character, in contrast, emphasize obedience to a set of central dogmas that are strongly enforced by government. When many moderns hear the term "religious character of society," they picture a culture based on religious freedom and strong religious behavior. But these are more likely in a commercial society because nations with a religious character are run by one church entity that controls government, media, education, business, travel, the military, and all other major aspects of society.

In fact, in nations operating under religious character, like Spain during the Inquisition or modern Iran under the Ayatollahs, there is very little freedom of religion, thought, finances, press, or belief.

People who profess a different religion are often, literally, put to death.

Such societies are divided between the masses and the agents of the religion (which include the military, police, and secret police), whose main purpose is to terrorize and force the people to do the mandates of the central church. This isn't religious freedom at all; it is actually the opposite. Again, the American founders rejected this as the ideal character for the new American nation.

Commercial societies provide a better character for freedom. Madison noted that commercial character is best for at least five reasons:

1. Commercial nations are more tolerant of religious freedoms and other differences, allowing for more freedom for all people.

2. Commercial nations are milder, meaning there is less violence (both at home and abroad) in commercial societies than in nations run by the military or one central church government.

3. Commercial societies are simply freer across the board.

4. In commercial societies, there is more social mobility for everyone, and class systems disappear in such nations.

5. In commercial societies, there is more economic mobility for everyone, meaning that anyone can work hard and achieve increased levels of success.

Entrepreneurs and Freedom

In short, nations of commercial character naturally resonate with freedom, openness, widespread opportunity, and prosperity. Religious freedom and freedom of the press are widespread, and the openness of society allows people from all backgrounds to seek improvement and more success. The central theme of martial nations is *strength*. The central theme of nations organized around a single church government is *authority*. The central theme of commercial nations is *freedom*.

Modern readers sometimes struggle to understand the difference between these three characters of nations because we have been raised in our own nation where one of these characters is so strongly ingrained. For example, during a discussion of these three potential national characteristics, one executive raised his hand and argued that Rome was actually commercial and that the reason for its strong military was simply to protect its commercial strength. Of course, he was simply describing the modern United States and projecting it onto his view of Rome.

Those in the room who had read Gibbon's *The Decline and Fall of the Roman Empire* or other great works of history tried to show him the differences, but it just didn't make sense to him. His whole life had been lived in a Western culture steeped in the commercial character, and he saw everything in those terms.

Finally, in exasperation, another executive in the room asked, "Have you ever seen any of the *Star Trek* movies?"

The first executive responded, "Well, I'm certainly not a Trekkie, but yes, I have seen a few movies and episodes."

"Okay," said the second executive, "then I have one word for you: Klingons."

A light came on in the first executive's mind. He finally got it. "Ohhhhhhh," he said.

There are cultures that literally care nothing about money except how it can increase their martial strength, who raise their children to be strong above all and build their entire society around war. From Attila the Hun to modern North Korea, such societies are real. Again, it can be difficult to grasp the other national characters when most of us have been raised in just one of these societies.

Note that there are two major branches of the commercial character in society. One is Mercantilism and the other is Free Enterprise. In mercantilist nations like historical Britain and modern Japan, the government owns many of the businesses and drives most of the economy, while in free-enterprise countries, the government protects the rights of the people from foreign attack and domestic crime and otherwise leaves the people free to create, build, and lead businesses and the overall economy.

Hamilton originally wanted America to be mercantilist with a few wealthy families and corporations owning most of the wealth and the rest of the nation working for these elites as their employees. He thought this arrangement would be best for the new United States because it would be able to directly compete with mercantilist Britain.

Jefferson disagreed with Hamilton's view, arguing that a nation made up of small business owners would have more freedom and would spread opportunity and prosperity to everyone rather than limiting the wealth to a few elites. Fortunately for the United States, the founding generation went with Jefferson's vision of Free Enterprise rather than Hamilton's Mercantilism.

The Values of Freedom

Americans, Canadians, and many of the European nations chose the free-enterprise commercial character for their societies because it is naturally connected to freedom and prosperity. Furthermore, free-enterprise commercial societies have certain values that strengthen freedom and prosperity over time.

Such values, as outlined by writers from Hesiod and Virgil to Alfred J. Nock and Allen Carlson, include:

- Self-sufficiency
- Limited government
- Government overseen by the people
- A free-enterprise legal system structured around private ownership
- Putting the needs of families ahead of the needs of institutions or government
- A suspicion of the military-industrial establishment
- The importance of local communities and regional identity

- The necessity of religious faith and religious freedom as a source of widespread virtue
- The unique power of marriage to maintain society

In free-enterprise commercial societies, entrepreneurs and small business owners are vital promoters of these values. *As small business goes, so go freedom and prosperity.* This is a historical law in free nations because the entrepreneurial values are the values of freedom.

Sadly, the free-enterprise commercial values are in decline in the modern United States, Canada, and beyond. In fact, the 1913 and 1936 events in the U.S. moved America swiftly in the direction away from Free Enterprise and toward Mercantilism. Indeed, many elites have long wanted America to be more like the mercantilist nations of Europe. This shift has only accelerated in recent years.

We need a revolution of entrepreneurship in the current United States, Canada, Europe, and around the world. Successful entrepreneurs are self-made and see the need to combine knowledge with action. Nations seeking freedom need to emphasize the traditional entrepreneurial values of innovation, initiative, ingenuity, tenacity, and adaptability. A return to these values at all levels of our society would jumpstart leadership, entrepreneurialism, freedom, and prosperity.

> *We need a revolution of entrepreneurship in the current United States, Canada, Europe, and around the world.*

The growing *Global Achievement Gap* in our schools, as outlined by Tony Wagner's book of this title, presents an ominous warning for Americans. Wagner argues that American schools are not just failing, but are obsolete. They therefore cannot prepare American workers for the new economy unless fundamental and drastic changes are instituted. We can change things if we choose, Wagner says, by adopting the values of critical thinking, agility, adaptability, initiative, curiosity, imagination, and entrepreneurialism, among others, in our school curriculum.

Secretary of Education Arne Duncan quoted Wagner in *Foreign Affairs*, saying that "the same skills needed for success in the global economy are those which make our economy vibrant and safe." He also foreshadowed the decades ahead by quoting President Barack Obama: "The nation that out-educates us today is going to out-compete us tomorrow."

> *"The nation that out-educates us today is going to out-compete us tomorrow."*

An Innovation Nation

Our nation desperately needs an innovation generation—an entrepreneurial revolution that brings a return to a true spirit of free enterprise. As shown above, the values of entrepreneurialism are the values of freedom; the success of one naturally promotes the success of the other.

To qualify for leadership in the Turning Point of Freedom ahead, become a successful leader and entrepreneur. The very act of successful entrepreneurship spreads and promotes the values and principles of free enterprise. In fact, successful entrepreneurs positively impact the future of freedom and prosperity even if they never get involved directly in changing society.

On the other hand, entrepreneurs who go beyond building their business and engage in making an additional impact on community leadership and societal government, either by funding good candidates and causes or by directly using their influence and leadership to improve governments at all levels, are desperately needed. The future of freedom may literally be in the hands of such leaders.

Furthermore, those who become successful entrepreneurs naturally learn the values upon which freedom is based. In so doing, they qualify themselves and those they influence to help lead their nation in the right direction.

Today's Challenge

There are two great modern visions of how to help our economy grow and flourish. One holds that the government is the center of economic prosperity (modern Mercantilism); the other believes in innovation from the free market (Free Enterprise). The first attempts to tax and spend; the second believes in the power of entrepreneurialism.

Gary Shapiro outlined in his book *The Comeback* what Washington needs to do to truly bring the U.S. economy back. This includes:

- Stop penalizing investments in start-ups.

- Direct any public funding of start-ups by private investors, not by government bureaucrats.
- Let any company fail according to the rules of the free market.
- Make economics, business, and entrepreneurial studies part of the public school curriculum.
- Ensure that business tax rates are transparent and predictable.
- Change tax laws to favor investment over debt.
- Reform immigration to encourage entrepreneurial risk-taking.
- Pass more free-trade agreements.
- Reform education by allowing teachers to really teach.
- Measure all government spending by how well it is actually working.
- Measure all government spending by how it meets serious national needs.
- Link the compensation of our federal legislators to our annual national deficit.

All of this amounts to a modern shift away from increasing Mercantilism and back to true Free Enterprise. Shapiro ultimately pins the future of America (and by extension, other national economies) on innovation and entrepreneurial leadership, not on either major political party or on any government policy. The government can do much to encourage a flourishing economy, but the innovators will primarily determine our economic future. Shapiro writes:

> Innovation *is* America. It is our special sauce, our destiny, and our best and only hope for escaping the economic malaise…Our best hope is for government to foster innovation by creating a fertile ground for innovation to flourish.
>
> Innovation is the natural by-product of the free market…
>
> Our nation is looking into the abyss. With a blinding focus on the present, our government is neglecting a future that demands thoughtful action. The only valid government action is that which invests in our children. This requires hard choices. We cannot leave the rising generation with a mountain of bad debt. This will require suffering in the present…
>
> America is in crisis. What is required is a commitment to innovation and growth. We can and must succeed. With popular and political resolve, we can reverse America's decline…America must become the world's innovative engine once again; we cannot fail. Only then can I return to China and tell that Communist Chinese official that America is back.

Shapiro is correct that the voice of innovation and free enterprise is vital to America's future. And indeed the same is true of any nation that desires to be free and prosperous. Unless we find ways to reinvigorate innovation, the future of our economy and nation is

bleak. Two centuries of American leadership have proven that freedom works. It's time to remember and more vigorously apply freedom in our modern economy. It's time to return to freedom and to
let entrepreneurs do their magic.

It is unlikely, however, that such a change will occur without the
direct leadership of more successful entrepreneurs in our society.
With this said, it is clear that we have a problem, and a big one. As
an optimist, I am usually skeptical of anything that sounds overly
negative. However, "Harper's Index" recently listed several statistics
that are cause for serious concern. A few items on the list received
very little press:

- Percentage of Americans in 2009 who believed the free market "is the best system on which to base the future of the
  world": 74
- Percentage of Americans who believe so today [2011]: 59
- Percentage of Chinese who do: 67

If this trend continues, we'll face drastically worsening major
problems. Unease about the growth of China's power has been increasing in the U.S. for some time. But the concern has mostly cen-
tered on America's economic decline versus the growth of China as
a major totalitarian world power. Add to this the knowledge that
over two-thirds of Chinese believe free enterprise is the key to the
future—at the same time that American belief in free enterprise is
waning—and our sense of what the twenty-first century will bring

takes on a new direction.

In the United States, youth are widely taught that the key to life and career success is getting a good job, while in China an emphasis for the "best and brightest" in the rising generation is to engage meaningful innovation, technology, invention, and entrepreneurship. If this continues, the status and roles of these two nations will literally switch in the decades ahead: China as superpower, the U.S. as a second-rate nation with a stagnant and struggling economy. Many experts point out that China has a long way to go to "catch up" with the U.S. in military strength, but how long will this take if the U.S. economy continues to decline while China's booms under entrepreneurial leadership?

I have two main thoughts on this: First, good for the Chinese people! If they can consistently nudge their society and government in the direction of increased freedom, they will join or possibly even become the world's most important leaders. The truth is that freedom works—and it can work in China as well as everywhere else. Second, and most importantly, America, Canada, and other Western nations need a return to a focus on free enterprise.

The future of our freedom and prosperity depends on a flourishing environment of freedom. Government can do us all a great service by altering its current policies and removing the numerous obstacles to free enterprise. This one significant shift is vital. The fact that many of our national leaders seem committed to avoiding such changes is a big problem. The longer this lasts, the bigger the problem becomes. It is likely that such changes can only be made by the leadership of successful entrepreneurs.

The Power of Entrepreneurs

In fact, the power of entrepreneurs beyond business is a vitally important historical reality. Free citizens are innovative, independent, and giving. When these characteristics wane in a society, freedom decreases. When these values are bolstered, freedom grows. Because they are so important in free nations, institutions attempt to produce and market them. But the nature of innovation, independence, and giving make them resistant to Institutionalism and Mercantilism; when big institutions take over these values, they slowly (sometimes more quickly) begin to disappear, and freedom goes with them.

Such shifts come in both evolutionary and cyclical patterns. Each new age (Nomadic, Agrarian, Industrial, Information) is forged and grows when the values of freedom flourish, levels off as they stagnate, and declines as they are lost among the citizenry and later from institutions. On a cyclical level, nations rise in power and prosperity as innovation, independence, and giving permeate the culture at the individual level. They weaken as individuals focus on other things and leave these values to institutions, and they move into periods of crisis when the institutions fail to deliver.

We are right now in an era of crisis because our big societal institutions are not effectively promoting the values of freedom or innovation. Crisis ruins societies where the citizens don't restore these values to their daily lives, while such crises are building blocks to growth and empowerment when the regular people re-adopt innovation, independence, and giving.

Governments try to speed things up by requiring and regulating these values, but this very act moves nations toward crisis. If the people are forced to innovate, creativity shuts down. Forced independence is dependence. And forced giving without the value of real charity is a form of enslavement.

Institutions are, at their best, designed to perpetuate the values of a society or group. But when the people lose values, the institutions themselves often become the enemy of these exact values.

Combining the Values

The American ideal of freedom and prosperity "through opportunity for all" is the basis of our greatest institutions—private and governmental. The American founding generation was made up of entrepreneurs, and they used their entrepreneurial skills and wisdom when they wrote the U.S. Constitution.

Perhaps the single greatest generational foray into entrepreneurial government gave us the U.S. Congress, presidency, Supreme Court and a republic of fifty sovereign and united states. These institutions were designed by an entrepreneurial generation, and the goal was, above all, to perpetuate a citizenry steeped in the values of freedom, including innovation, independence, and giving.

Today, those whose status or self-perception is based on ties to the institutional are mostly, by definition, caught in the culture of maintaining the status quo, dependence, and "getting." As a result, they often feel threatened by those whose culture centers on innovating, independence, and giving. From the perch of credibility, which institutions seek to bestow, the "experts" too often preach against innovation ("too risky"), independence ("obviously ignorant"), and giving ("too idealistic"). It is poignant that the same Establishment that says, "The upstarts must be put in their place, lest things change," also preaches that "The world is what it is, and you'll never change it." "It's just business." "Security is the name of the game." "Avoid risk at all costs."

Ironically, today's "Innovators" don't see the "Maintainers" as enemies or competitors, just as allies who have yet to grasp reality. Things change. Or more accurately, all things change. The Maintainers are fighting it, while the Innovators set out to lead it. But only entrepreneurship can make this happen.

The irony of this all is that to survive and flourish, the Establishment needs innovation and entrepreneurship. Power and wealth can be held by a dominating aristocracy or upper class, but the masses suffer and prosperity declines. Without an independent and giving citizenry, no nation can long remain free or generally prosperous.

For freedom and prosperity to flourish, the freedom values must be actively applied by the regular people engaging in entrepreneurial behaviors. And in times like ours, they frequently must do so without much leadership from the big institutions.

Nations which accomplish this are worthy of the freedom they create and pass on to posterity. It is up to the regular people: We must exemplify innovation, independence, and giving. The future of our nation will be determined by this reality. The future of freedom will be decided by entrepreneurs.

CHAPTER 9

Solution #2: Voracious Readers and Independent Thinkers

The second thing that qualifies a person to be a leader in the coming Turning Point is becoming a voracious reader and an independent thinker. Together, wide and deep reading along with innovative thinking creates not only leaders, but the kind of leaders who build freedom.

> *Together, wide and deep reading along with innovative thinking creates not only leaders, but the kind of leaders who build freedom.*

Once when I was teaching a graduate course on the *Federalist Papers*, I became frustrated that some students didn't read the assigned studies before class. When questioned, they said the readings weren't very interesting, and they preferred to just come to class and listen to me explain the various writings from the *Federalist*.

I gave some thought to how to get them more excited about reading, and then I suspended the assignments for several days and had them read *The Gulag Archipelago* by Aleksandr Solzhenitsyn.

This turned out to be very effective. As they read the dozens of stories of how the Soviet government and bureaucracy treated its citizens, they became emotional and, in more than a few cases, deeply upset with what the loss of freedom meant to Russian citizens. When a few students raised their hands in class and asked why I would assign such depressing readings about the results of tyranny in a society, I simply held up *Gulag* in one hand and said, "If you don't like this…" Then I held up the *Federalist* in another hand and said, "…then you better read this—one or the other."

After that, they read the *Federalist* closely and on time and came to class excited to discuss freedom. The principles of freedom aren't particularly exciting to many people, but when they experience the loss of freedom (personally or by proxy), this quickly changes. Freedom is a primary good: We all want it, and in fact, we all need it (see Chapter 11).

> *The principles of freedom aren't particularly exciting to many people, but when they experience the loss of freedom (personally or by proxy), this quickly changes.*

I have repeated this process many other times when I taught classes or seminars on the *Federalist Papers*, the Constitution, or Tocqueville, and it has always left readers more excited about freedom. In fact, if you have a hard time making yourself study the fine print of our government and societal documents, try starting by reading *The Gulag Archipelago*. (I recommend the one-volume abridged version edited by Edward E. Ericson, Jr.)

The loss of freedom is a great tragedy in any society, but especially to a society whose focus has been freedom for over two centuries.

Historical Models

The freest nations of history, from Ancient Israel and Athens to the free Swiss, are famous for how widespread and intense the level of reading and independent debate was in their societies.

The American founding generation followed this pattern. The founders cared deeply about freedom because they read, and they read because they cared deeply about freedom.

Just consider what Samuel Williams, a Harvard professor in the American founding era, said about the average education of American children in 1794:

> All the children are trained up to this kind of knowledge: they are accustomed from their earliest years to read the Holy Scriptures, the periodical publications, newspapers, and political pamphlets; to form some general acquaintance with the laws of their country, the proceedings of the courts of justice, of the general assembly of the state, and of the Congress, etc.
>
> Such a kind of education is common and universal in every part of the state: and nothing would be more dishonorable to the parents, or to the children, than to be without it.

Such people were deep readers. And the freedoms they fought for showed it.

Leaders are readers. This is true in business, in many areas of society, and certainly for citizens of nations that remain free. Leaders are readers, and leaders are also independent and innovative thinkers.

Calvin Coolidge: A Great Example

One example of a voracious reader and independent, innovative thinker is President Calvin Coolidge. In the aftermath of the changes that came in 1913, very few took notice of the negative World Shift. During the immediate years after 1913, World War I dominated the North American and European narrative.

In a break from this trend, Calvin Coolidge realized how problematic the new changes were and decided to do something about it. He spoke out, ran for office, served as president of the United States, and worked to help return the nation to its roots of freedom. He was not fully successful, mainly because by the time he took action, the World Shift had already occurred, but his voice did help slow the onslaught of massive government.

Ironically, Coolidge's opponents labeled him with the nickname "Silent Cal Coolidge," and most schoolchildren today, if they hear about Coolidge at all, learn that President Coolidge said little and did little as president. In reality, he was a strong proponent of free government against the Wilsonian model, which began in 1913.

Coolidge said a number of things that are still highly relevant today. For example:

"This [change in America] has not been accomplished without what is virtually a change in the form, and actually a change in process, of our government...The outcome of this doctrine has been the adoption of the...direct election of the United States senators...This is not the government which was put into form by Washington and Hamilton, and popularized by Jefferson."

"A people gather, grow strong under adversity, weaken under prosperity, and fall, first victims of weakness within and then victims of strength without. No one can deny this."

"All the elaborate functions of the government will be of no avail, unless there abide in the people the simple homely virtues of industry and thrift, honesty and charity...All of our natural resources, all of our attempted industrial organization, all of our guarantees of freedom will avail nothing without the support of character. There can be no national greatness which does not rest upon the personal integrity of the people."

"But if our republic is to be maintained and improved it will be through the efforts and character of the individual. It will be, first of all, because of the influences which exist in the home, for it is the ideals which prevail in the home life which make up the strength of the nation."

"There can be no society without a home, and no civilization without citizenship."

"The attempt to regulate, control, and prescribe all manner of conduct and social relations is very old…Such governments assumed jurisdiction over the action, property, life, and even religious convictions of their citizens down to the minutest detail. A large part of the history of free institutions is the history of the people struggling to emancipate themselves from this bondage."

"As the standard of civilization rises there is a necessity for a larger and larger outlay to maintain the cost of existence. As the activities of government increase, as it extends its field of operations, the initial tax which it requires becomes manifolded many times…When there is added to this aggravated financial condition an increasing amount of regulation…the burden of it all becomes very great."

"A sound and wise statesmanship which recognizes and attempts to abide by [the Constitution's] limitations will undoubtedly find itself displaced by that type of public official who promises much, talks much, legislates much, expends much, but accomplishes little."

"[America should have a] system where the individual is clothed with inalienable rights, the people are supreme, and the government is their agent. Under this conception there is real freedom, real independence and grave personal responsibility. The rulers look to the people. Their authority is the public will, ascertained in accordance with law. There will be the least possible interference with private affairs.

"Realizing that it is the people who support the government and not the government which supports the people, there will be no resort to paternalism. Under such institutions there may appear to be a lack of machine-like efficiency, but there will be no lack of character. Private initiative will be stimulated. Self-reliance and self-control will be increased… This is the ideal of America."

"One of the chief errors of our present day is that of relying too much on government and too little on our own efforts and on the people themselves. This comes to pass by supposing that, when there is something which ought to be done, we can avoid all personal responsibility by a simple ordinance requiring that hereafter it shall be done by government."

"Individual initiative, in the long run, is a firmer reliance than bureaucratic supervision…We do not need more knowledge; we need more character. We do not need more government; we need more culture. We do not need more law; we need more religion. We do not need more of the things that are seen; we need more of the things that are unseen…If the foundation be firm, the superstructure will stand."

"There is no place for the cynic or the pessimist. Who is he that can take no part in business because he believes it is selfish? Who is he that can take no part in religion because he believes it is imperfect? These institutions are the instruments by which an eternal purpose is working out the salvation of the world. It is not for us to regard them with disdain; it is for us to work with them, to dedicate ourselves to them, to justify our faith in them."

"We have been successful beyond others in great commercial and industrial enterprises because we have been a people of vision. Our prosperity has resulted not by disregarding but by maintaining high ideals. Material resources do not, and cannot, stand alone; they are the product of spiritual resources."

Perhaps the greatest lesson we can learn from Coolidge is to take action during the time of a great World Shift. Once the shift has come, it is usually too late to stop it.

Better Citizens Needed

A significant part of the problem is that for at least three generations, young Americans have been taught to leave governance to the
experts. In the educational focus on
career training, which became the
norm in the 1930s, the idea of each
citizen truly understanding our government, freedoms, and the principles
of prosperity has almost disappeared.

> *A significant part of the problem is that for at least three generations, young Americans have been taught to leave governance to the experts.*

We expect the experts to keep the
economy strong, and as a nation, we
are more focused on our own specific
jobs. The loss of the idea that each citizen needs the same quality of
education as every governor, senator, president, or CEO has taken its
toll on our freedoms and prosperity.

We want our political leaders to know all the issues, but we give
our citizens—the overseers of our freedoms, and the grantors of
the powers our government wields—permission to know very little
about freedom and the economy.

Yet it is precisely these citizens who elect our leaders. Many
Americans worry that we need better congressmen, judges, or presi-
dents, but free societies flourish when they have better citizens.
Again, the ideal is for each average citizen to have the kind of educa-

tion that our presidents or governors enjoy.

We are far from this ideal. For example, fewer than half of Americans aged 18-24 surveyed could point out New York, Ohio, or Iraq on a map. Fully 88 percent could not point out Afghanistan on a map, even though our war there is the longest war in U.S. history. Twenty-eight percent of Americans believe the population of the United States exceeds one billion people.

A *National Geographic* study found that when asked which language has the most native speakers, three-fourths of young Americans answered "English"; the correct answer is Mandarin Chinese. Note that the second most popular major native language is Spanish; English is third, and Arabic is fourth.

An Intercollegiate Studies Institute study found that less than half of Americans (of all ages) could name all three branches of government. In a 2010 study, two-thirds of Americans could not name a single Supreme Court Justice. And in a 2009 study of American adults, more people "knew that Michael Jackson sang 'Beat It' than knew that the Bill of Rights is part of the U.S. Constitution."

There are many similar examples. It goes without saying that it is very difficult to be the kind of citizen-leaders that promote and spread freedom without such basic knowledge.

A Widespread International Challenge

Nor is the United States alone in this troubling trend of poor civic knowledge. For example, another leading free nation, Canada, provides a significant case study of how widespread this problem is in modern democracies. A 2007 Dominion Institute study "found that 80% of Canadians aged 18 to 24 failed a simple 30-question 'exam' about Canadian history. Just one quarter (26%) knew the year of Confederation."

A study by the Canadian Policy Research Networks concluded:

> Knowing the names of major political leaders and contenders, how Parliament functions, how social policies have been implemented in the past and basic historical facts about Canada and global affairs are all forms of civic liberty that elude a large number of Canadians...
>
> Young Canadians lack both sufficient knowledge of how government works and the capacity to apply democratic skills beyond their school walls...[Y]oung Canadians are less knowledgeable about politics than any other age group in the country, and perhaps more disturbingly, by a wider margin today than ten years ago.
>
> One study from a high school in Ottawa is indicative of the problem:
>
> On the over 80 questionnaires completed by students, less than 30% named a citizenship lesson in school that dealt with specific political content...During interviews, most students struggled to recall the basic political facts of their courses.
>
> Many other studies indicate that students do not have a

firm grasp of key political terms…[F]ew youth could define a central concept like "democracy"…Other focus groups…in New Brunswick recorded a team of young women who gave the following definition of democracy: "We aren't sure, but we thought it wasn't a good thing. We don't think we have it here in Canada. We think it is when you don't have the right to give your ideas, like in Russia or in Germany with Hitler."

Apparently, such confusion was commonplace, as most respondents sympathized with each other's confusion. Based on [this] study and other international research, this last response would seem like a worst-case scenario, albeit surely not unique.

These studies are indicative of similar findings in Western Europe, Japan, and other participatory democracies. Clearly freedom is under siege in all free nations, since the ultimate source of freedom is always the wisdom of the people.

While much of the focus of this book is on the United States, the same types of trends are occurring across the free world, and the solutions discussed in this book are applicable in all free nations.

Change Needed

If we are going to regain our freedoms and culture of prosperity, things must change. Our textbooks have been "dumbed down" for at least three generations, and as long as we rely on official education for our learning, this problem will continue.

Indeed, as John Taylor Gatto, New York State Teacher of the Year in 1991, put it, the real lessons teachers too often teach in our schools are things like "Confusion," "Class Position," and "Mindless Obedience to Officials." C.S. Lewis pointed out this same trend in Britain in his excellent book *The Abolition of Man*.

Today, we desperately need a generation of citizens and voters who realize what is happening, understand just how rare and precious freedom is, and take action to restore our freedoms. To become such people, we need to read and think in the tradition of the American founding generations. We need to become nations of citizens who learn to read, analyze, innovate, and get effectively involved in leading society.

CHAPTER 10

Solution #3: Tribal Leaders

The third thing that qualifies one to lead in the major challenges ahead is to become a tribal leader. In current best-selling business literature, the concept of tribes has become a huge topic. Seth Godin's best-selling book *Tribes* argues that the business leaders of the near future, even now in fact, will learn to be tribal leaders. Another term for this same concept is community leader. We need to build many new communities to bring back real freedom and prosperity to our society.

Unlike the old-style communities and tribes, the new communities aren't limited by geographical boundaries. The Internet and other technologies have made it possible and popular for communities to arise naturally based on shared goals, ideas, and other factors. Nearly everyone is now part of several new communities or tribes— online or in some other way.

This trend seems poised to spread a lot more in the years ahead.

And as communities arise, there is more and more opportunity for leadership and positive influence. In fact, Godin says that all of us need to be leaders in this new tribal environment.

In a very real sense, technology has brought a return to the type of daily involvement that existed in the American founding era.

The Changing Place of Leadership

Of course, not everyone uses the new communities for political or economic purposes, but a lot do. And even those new tribes that are neither political nor economic in nature can be used to build community and promote the principles of freedom and prosperity.

At one point in the history of free nations, the leaders were mostly landowners and merchants. Later, society changed, and the top arenas of leadership were found in the professions: Most community elders were doctors, lawyers, and other professionals.

When society shifted again, managers became the top leaders. William Whyte's famous classic *The Organizational Man* detailed this era.

In the 1980s, various authors promoted another shift, this time from management to leadership. In this leadership revolution, authors like Warren Bennis and Stephen Covey taught leaders to focus more on doing the right things rather than just doing things right.

Today we are witnessing another such shift, from leadership in a given institution to tribal and community leadership in society. The new leaders succeed by building community, by supporting people in their areas of success, and by helping diverse people learn to work together toward common goals. This is the new tribal leader.

Another, more simple, way to describe tribal leadership is this: *leaders who build community by setting the example of successful entrepreneurship, voracious reading and independent thinking, and helping others do the same.*

It isn't enough just to be successful and wise. Leaders are readers, leaders are independent thinkers, and leaders are successful. Leaders keep trying until they find success, even when the path is difficult. But more than this, true leaders don't do it alone. They help others do the same. They set the example, yes, but they go further: They encourage others and help build communities of such leaders.

This is powerful and profound leadership. It takes the concept of leader to a whole new level.

The Most Important Concept of Freedom

I was once asked, "What is the most important thing Americans need to know right now about freedom?" I didn't even have to think about the answer.

I have shared this idea before, but it bears repeating. On many occasions, I have asked advanced graduate students or executives to diagram the American government model which established unprecedented levels of freedom and prosperity to people from all backgrounds, classes, and views.

They always do it in the wrong order, and they get the most important part wrong. Specifically, they start by diagramming three branches of government, a judicial and an executive and a bicameral legislature, and then they sit down. They think they've done the assignment.

When I ask, "What about the rest?" they are stumped for a few seconds. Then some of them have an epiphany and quickly return to the white board to diagram the same thing at the state level. This time, they are sure they are done.

"What level of government came first in the American colonies?" I ask. After some debate, they agree that many towns, cities, counties, and local governments were established, most with written constitutions, for over two centuries before the U.S. Constitution and many decades before the state governments and constitutions.

"So, diagram the founding model of local government," I say. They invariably diagram a copy of the three-branch U.S. constitutional model. This is entirely incorrect.

This sad lack of knowledge indicates at least one thing: Americans who have learned about our constitutional model have tended to learn it largely by rote, without truly understanding the foundational principles of freedom. We know about the three branches, the checks and balances, and we consider this the American political legacy. But few Americans today understand the principles and deeper concepts behind the three branches, checks, and balances.

The first constitutions and governments in America were local, and there were hundreds of them. These documents were the basis of later state constitutions, and they were also the models in which early Americans learned to actively govern themselves.

Without them, the state constitutions could never have been written. Without these local and state constitutions, the U.S. Constitution would have been very, very different. In short, these local constitutions and governments were, and are, the basis of American freedoms and the whole system.

> *These local constitutions and governments were, and are, the basis of American freedoms and the whole system.*

The surprising thing, at least to many moderns, is that these local constitutions were very different than the state and federal constitutional model. There were some similarities, but the structure was drastically different. The principles of freedom are applied differently to be effective at local and tribal levels. A society that doesn't understand this is unlikely to stay free. Indeed, history is clear on this point.

Another surprise is that nearly all the early townships and cities in the Americas adopted a very similar constitutional structure. They were amazingly alike. This is because they are designed to apply the best principles of freedom to the local and tribal levels.

And there is more. This similar model was followed by the Iroquois League as well, and by several other First Nation tribal governments. Many people have heard this, but few can explain the details of how local free governments were established.

This same model of free local/tribal government shows up in tribes throughout Central and South America, Oceana, Africa, Asia, and the historic Germanic tribes, including the Anglo Saxons. Indeed, it is found in the Bible as followed by the Tribes of Israel. This is where the American founders said they found it.

The most accurate way, then, to diagram the American governmental system is to diagram the local system correctly and then the state and federal levels with their three branches each, separations of power, and checks and balances. But how exactly does one diagram the local level?

The Basics of Freedom

The basics are as follows. The true freedom system includes establishing as the most basic unit of society—next to the family— small government councils that are small enough to include all adults in the decision-making meetings for major choices.

This system is clearly described in Tocqueville's *Democracy in America*, Volume 1, Chapter 5, and in Liberty Fund's *Colonial Origins of the American Constitutions*. It is also portrayed in the classic television series *Little House on the Prairie* and in many books like Moody's *Little Britches,* Stratton-Porter's *Laddie* and James Fenimore Cooper's *Last of the Mohicans*. In fact, if you know to look for it, it shows up throughout much of human history.

These adult town, city, or tribal councils truly establish and maintain freedom by including in the most local and foundational decisions the voices and votes of all the adult citizenry. These councils make decisions by majority vote after open discussion. They also appoint mayors/chiefs, law enforcement leaders, judges, and other personnel. All of these officials report directly to the full council of all adults and can be removed by the council.

Where representative houses and offices are much more effective at the larger state and national levels, the whole system breaks down if the regular citizens aren't actively involved in governance at the most local levels. In this model, every adult citizen is formally a government official, with the result that all citizens study the government system, their role in it, the issues and laws and cases, and think like leaders.

> *The whole system breaks down if the regular citizens aren't actively involved in governance at the most local levels.*

They learn leadership by leading. Without this participatory government system at the local levels, as history has shown, freedom is eventually lost in all societies.

However, as we discussed earlier, it is nearly always a vital few that make all the difference. A few good leaders help everyone else do what is needed. Not everyone will engage the needed changes, but a few leaders can help things change. Such leadership starts with us!

Grassroots Leadership Is Necessary for Freedom to Flourish

Once again, the most successful tribes, communities, and even nations throughout history have adopted this model of local governance which includes all citizens in the basic local decision making. The result, in every society on record, has always been increased freedom and prosperity.

No free society in recorded history has maintained its great freedom once this system eroded. Tocqueville called this system of local citizen governance "the" most important piece of America's freedom model, and it was widespread in Canada as well.

Indeed, the U.S. Constitution is what it is because of the understanding the founding American generations gained from long participation in local government councils. These were the basis of state constitutions and the federal Constitution. If we don't understand the local councils, we don't understand the Constitution or freedom.

Today, we need a citizenship that truly understands freedom—not just patriotic, loyal, or highly professional people. This is the most important thing modern Americans can know if we want to maintain our freedom and widespread prosperity.

In addition to needing a return to such local councils, many leaders can learn such leadership through involvement in business organizations that train leaders and encourage more community interaction. Businesses that build communities of people working together to build leaders are especially helpful.

The Leaders of the Future

Every generation faces its share of great national challenges, and ours will certainly be no different. One of the challenges clearly ahead for us is the future of freedom. Our freedoms have been decreasing for some time, and the losses are more frequent now than ever before.

Twenty-five years from now, or some time close to that, each of us will have to look our children and grandchildren in the eyes and tell them one of two things. We will either have to tell them that we presided over the greatest loss of freedom in history, or that we took action to bring back freedom. Then we will send them home to their lives—lives of freedom…or not.

This is real. Freedom is rare. Freedom is precious. Freedom is being lost. And we *can* make a difference.

This is a challenge we can win. But we will only be up to it if we qualify by becoming successful, being voracious leaders and independent thinkers, and becoming tribal and community leaders who help many others become the leaders they were born to be.

Again, this is a challenge we can win. But it will only be won by doing the little things, the daily items that build successful businesses, the hours of reading that train minds for leadership, and the mentoring of others for their own successful leadership. It is up to us.

Freedom matters. It will win or lose in the years just ahead. A Turning Point is coming—either for freedom or against it.

What will we tell our grandchildren in twenty-five years? Will we be able to look them directly in the eyes and tell them that freedom won? We are making this decision now, day by

> *Freedom matters. It will win or lose in the years just ahead. A Turning Point is coming—either for freedom or against it.*

day, as we make choices about entrepreneurship, becoming truly educated, and building community.

What choice will *you* make today?

CHAPTER 11

Essential Freedom

"The experience of nations with well-being is exceedingly brief.
Nearly all, throughout history, have been very poor."
–John Kenneth Galbraith

Freedom matters. Freedom, like love, salt, and charisma, is hard to quantify, but we know it when we experience it.

Freedom is the essential element that makes it possible for us to choose whom to marry, how to raise our kids, how we'll worship, what level and type of education suits us, what we do for a living, etc. These are obvious to pretty much everyone and are the common man's definition of freedom. When these things are threatened, most people take notice and resist the influence that is interfering with their choices.

But there is a deeper reality to freedom, and it is at least as important as the right to choose these significant features in our lives. It is as subtle as the air we breathe—and as vital to our continued way of life. And because it is subtle, and so easily taken for granted, only the very vigilant few are aware that it is all but gone in our day.

More to the point, we will either lose our freedoms or win them back in the years just ahead. This may be the most important challenge of our generation.

What Is Freedom?

But what exactly is freedom? Why does it matter so much? And what would it be like to lose it? The answers reveal how little most moderns really know about this vital resource that makes all other success possible.

Freedom is a primary good. According to Aristotle, this means that freedom is a universal goal of all human beings and almost nobody can be happy without it.

In the Aristotelian view of the world (which was also discussed by great thinkers Plato, John Locke, and David Hume, among others), there are at least three major levels of things:

1. *Primary Goods* are things everyone wants for their own sake, simply because they are so valuable. There are only a few primary goods in the world, including love, freedom, friendship, and happiness.

2. *Secondary Goods* are things many people want because they tend to increase the likelihood of increasing one's amount of primary goods. Secondary goods include things like respect, wealth, power, purpose, health, talents, etc. People can live

without them, but most people don't want to.

3. *Tertiary Goods* are things some people want because they think these will bring them more secondary goods. This level of things includes items like a job, an academic degree, a handsome or beautiful face, an inheritance, a nice car or house, quality jewelry, etc. Such tertiary goods may or may not help a person get more respect, power, assets, or talents, but they are often valued because they might.

Of course, each person ranks things a little differently, but nearly all people need primary goods in order to live happy lives. Aristotle taught that primary goods are their own reward. But the reality is that a person who is happy, loved, and free is likely to increase his happiness, love, and freedom. Success breeds success.

Primary Goods

In short, a person with true freedom, happiness, and love is a successful person from any perspective. Even if he lacks wealth or power, who can argue that he is unsuccessful? After all, he is truly happy, free, and loved.

Moreover, because he is free, he can obtain whatever secondary and tertiary goods he may choose to seek. He has the freedom to obtain whatever he wants. Freedom allows one to engage in the pursuit of happiness.

In contrast, a person with wealth, power, talent, and health who isn't happy, loved, or free is clearly unsuccessful. No matter the size of his assets or power, he is unhappy, and his lack of freedom means he cannot improve his situation.

Put simply, freedom means one has the ability to improve his situation in life—whatever it may be. Without freedom, there is no chance of progress, except by first winning one's freedom and then using it to get what one wants in life.

> *Put simply, freedom means one has the ability to improve his situation in life— whatever it may be.*

If your dreams are more prosperity, more time with your family, more money to pay the bills, more free time for the hobbies you care about, a better house or car, to get in better shape, to increase the quality of your most important relationships, or anything else, your level of freedom will determine whether or not you can have what you want.

Three Kinds of Freedom

Freedom is a combination of political freedom, spiritual freedom, and financial freedom. When any of these is reduced, your ability to seek and have what you want for you or your family is decreased.

> *Freedom is a combination of political freedom, spiritual freedom, and financial freedom.*

Spiritual freedom is the highest of all—even the slave or prisoner can feel close to his God and clear in his conscience. On the other end of the scale, higher political and financial freedoms help one serve others and help raise the spiritual freedom of many.

Political freedom is lost when government fails to do its job or steps outside its proper roles. Spiritual freedom is lost when we lose faith or the ability to be inspired. Financial freedom is lost when we don't have (or misuse) the opportunity to increase our prosperity and fund our wants and dreams.

Human beings invented government with one purpose: to protect each person's political, spiritual, and economic freedoms. When government does its job correctly, it protects all citizens from foreign attackers and domestic criminals who want to take away their freedom.

Unfortunately, throughout history most governments have used their power to begin to reduce the political, spiritual, and financial freedom of their people. As Lord Acton noted, power corrupts, and absolute power corrupts absolutely.

When people are given the power of government position, very few can resist the temptation to use it to benefit themselves, which results in decreasing the freedoms of others.

How Rare Is Freedom?

Due to this reality, freedom is very rare in history—very rare. Only a few nations have maintained freedom for more than a generation. If we compare the nations of history to the freedoms outlined in *The Declaration of Independence*, for example, only a few nations in history have really been free.

These include ancient Israel, a brief period in the history of Athens, the Saracens, a brief time in the history of Switzerland and also France, the early Anglo-Saxons and various eras in British history, the United States, and a few others.

In all of these cases, freedom was eventually reduced. Unfortunately, freedom in the United States has been decreasing for many decades, just like the pattern of these earlier examples.

In addition to these few eras of historical freedom, a few tribal cultures in human history have managed a period of free society. But the total number of people in history who have experienced freedom at the levels we now enjoy adds up to much less than 1 percent of the world's population over time.

In fact, less than 1 percent of people in the world today benefit from the levels of political, spiritual, and financial freedom enjoyed by most American citizens during the 160 years from 1776 to 1936. All of us in our day have lost many of the freedoms our American forefathers experienced.

Of course, the American founding generations had their share of flaws. They withheld freedom from minorities; allowed and, in many places, embraced slavery; and, in a number of cases, followed class systems and gender relations in the backward traditions of Britain and other European nations.

But it was precisely the freedom gained by these generations that eventually led to the end of slavery and increased freedoms for all in later generations. Freedom through the Revolution and established long-term by the Constitution naturally spread and eventually created a lot more freedom for everyone.

Today, however, all of us are witnessing the reduction of our freedoms—and have been for decades. This is a human tragedy. And it is precisely those of us who benefit from relatively high levels of freedom today who too often take our freedoms for granted—and who misunderstand how rare and fragile a commodity freedom is.

When Freedom Is Lacking

It is difficult to realize how valuable something is when you have always had it and never lost it. But try imagining what you would lose if your freedoms were significantly decreased.

For example, the majority of people in the world today cannot openly worship and believe in the religion of their choice. If you lost this freedom, how would it change your life?

Likewise, many people in the world today cannot have as many children as they choose. The number is regulated by their government, and police officers come to their homes and enforce abortions beyond the legal number of pregnancies. These kind of horror stories out of China over the last four decades should remind us all of how precious, and fragile, freedom is. How would such a loss of freedom impact your dreams and happiness?

Many parents in today's world are required to raise their children according to extremely intrusive government regulations, inspections, and oversight on each family. Such governmental behavior is not limited to the Nazi era across much of Europe, the Saddam Hussein era in Iraq, or modern-day Syrian or African dictatorships. Such abuses of power have taken place in nations such as modern Germany. How would you feel about such a development in your family?

This list goes on and on. Most Americans, Canadians, and Europeans have no idea how widely freedom is restricted around the world.

For example, many people in today's world do not get to choose their own career path. What job they'll have, how much they get paid, and what town and apartment they live in are determined by government-administered exams and the quotas of government bureaucrats. In nations as seemingly free as Spain and France, for example, student exams determine far too much about their lives. This is at times a problem in the United States and Canada as well.

Governments often determine whether or not citizens can have a car, what kind of car they get and how much fuel they can use, whether they can buy or own jewelry, what the jewelry is made of and looks like, what they can talk about with their spouse or children, what things they can never say to a spouse or child, who they can marry and when…the list is extensive. This is real. *This is the world we live in.*

For example, a few years ago a friend of mine landed a job with a new Asian-owned car factory opening in North America. Imagine his surprise when he was handed a list of instructions outlining what cars he could drive, what size of house he could own, and what schools his children could attend.

This type of structuring of employee lives, even outside of the workplace, is the norm for workers in many seemingly free nations around the world. We expect it in Russia and China, but it surprises us when it shows up in South Korea, Japan, Sweden, or the United States. When private businesses become this intrusive, freedom suffers, but when government does this (and too many do), it is a direct attack on freedom.

Freedom is incredibly rare. It is rare in the modern world, and it is even more rare when compared to the generations of humans through history. Freedom is rarer than friendship, happiness, love, and the other primary goods. Freedom, in the context of the billions of human beings who have been born in the world, is rarer than diamonds and gold.

Do We Realize?

The biggest danger to freedom may be that free people are usually unaware of just how valuable, rare, and fragile freedom is until they lose it. In many years of signing books and shaking hands at big conventions, I have had dozens of immigrants from nations lacking freedom thank me, while weeping, for the work I do to promote freedom. Such convention attendees have come from Russia, Eastern Europe, Latin America, Africa, and China. But I have had almost no such conversations with natural-born American citizens or Canadians and only a few from Western Europe. Such a concept just doesn't cross our minds as much as it does for those who have lived without freedom; we breathe freedom, and we often take it for granted.

We Westerners seem to have little idea of just how precious freedom is and just how much we would miss it if we lost it. At the same time, like the proverbial frog in the kettle, we are too often oblivious to the rate at which America's freedoms are being reduced every year. The current drain of freedom may be the most important trend of our current world. Yet far too few of us take notice.

We are losing our freedoms. This has been happening for a long time, but the pace is increasing and we are running out of time to reverse this trend. And prosperity is decreasing along with freedom. As Stephen Marche put it in his *Esquire* article "We Are Not All Created Equal": "There are some truths so hard to face, so ugly, and so at odds with how we imagine the world should be, that nobody can accept them. Here's one: It is obvious that a class system has arrived in America—a recent study of the thirty-four countries in the Organization for Economic Cooperation and Development found that only Italy and Great Britain have less social mobility. But nobody wants to admit: If your daddy was rich, you're gonna stay rich, and if your daddy was poor, you're gonna stay poor."

> *"There are some truths so hard to face, so ugly, and so at odds with how we imagine the world should be, that nobody can accept them."*

The most effective way around this trend is successful entrepreneurship, but for most Americans, the new class divide is the reality. When freedom decreases, so does prosperity. In modern America, both are in decline for most people.

The American Dream has historically meant that one generation expected a better standard of living for their children and grand-children. Few today have confidence in such a future. In fact, many Americans believe that their own children will likely have a lower standard of living than they do, but that the youth in China will have a higher standard of living than their parents.

I believe America has a bright future—if a few committed citi-zens rise up and become successful entrepreneurs, become truly educated, and lead communities.

CHAPTER 12

Free Citizens Read the Fine Print

"If you have built castles in the air, your work need not be lost; that is where they should be. Now put the foundations under them."
—Henry David Thoreau

Freedom is not a complex idea. But we do live in a complex world, and only complex government forms have proven able to keep those with power from exerting too much of it.

The American founders mixed the simple and the complex. Following the suggestions of great classical writers like Polybius, Montesquieu, and Hume, they pitted power against power, institution against institution, authority against authority—the Senate against the House, the Congress against the presidency, the courts against the Congress, the states against the federal government, and so on. And they put the people in charge of it all.

The details *are* complex. The House represents the people and, by extension, the poor. The Senate represents the states and also, naturally, the wealthy. The president represents the nation. The court represents the Constitution. The states represent themselves, but also the people.

The Constitution represents itself; the people just have to read and apply it. It also represents the people—it is written by them to the government, outlining limits of what the government may and may not do. The electors in the Electoral College, which elects the president, also represent the people. This is the way it stood originally.

In simple terms, the following were represented once: the wealthy and the nation. On the complex side, those which were naturally less powerful than the wealthy and national government were represented twice: the states and also the Constitution.

The least naturally powerful group, the regular people, was represented in our constitutional model four times (by the House, the local and state governments, the document of the Constitution itself, and the power to oversee the entire system and change it).

This is complex in design, but what could be more simple than a government by, for, and of the people?

On the side of complexity, the founders mixed the ideas of Polybius, Montesquieu, Hume, Blackstone, Adam Smith, and others in this process. On the side of simplicity, the people simply need to read the Constitution and the great freedom classics to understand freedom.

Who's to Blame?

Another simple reality is this: When people lose their freedoms in such a system, it is always the people, not the system, which have failed. The people have all the power, but they must choose to exercise it.

If the people understand freedom, read history and the Constitution and the great political and economic classics, and stay actively involved in maintaining their freedoms, the complex arrangement of constitutional freedoms will not fail.

But when the people turn to other matters and neglect to maintain their freedoms, when they allow the Seventeenth Amendment or *United States v. Butler* or the insertion of party politics into the government, for example, to reduce the power of the people, it becomes more difficult for later generations to promote freedom. Still, the Constitution is there, and a wise citizenry has the power to reboot American freedom.

When the understanding of the citizens is simple, the actions they must take to be free are complex—even confusing or overwhelming. When the understanding of the citizens is complex, the actions they must take are simple.

Vital Foundations of Freedom

Next to learning how to become more involved in community and societal leadership, one of the most important things we need in this nation is more citizens who read the fine print—of the Constitution, historical documents and cases, and current bills and government policies. Canada and many free nations have the same problem.

To begin with, there are a few things which are fundamentally vital to the success and maintenance of the U.S. Constitution. If these vital things are lost or ignored, or even changed, the system will break down, and our freedoms will decrease. These vital foundations include:

- Separations of power among the executive, legislative, and judicial branches
- The independence of each branch
- Checks and balances
- No *ex post facto* laws (laws passed and applied retroactively so that something that is legal today may become illegal next week and you may be arrested and prosecuted for doing it even when it was legal)
- No bills of attainder (laws directed at specific citizens)
- The right to not be held by the government without being charged and having a warrant issued
- The various other vital freedoms outlined in the Bill of Rights
- Separation of power between the federal and state governments

Over the years, some have argued that we are in danger of losing some of these vital foundations of constitutional freedom. Certainly there has been some weakening over time. But for the most part, the vital facets of the Constitution have held strong.

Weakening the Constitution

Unfortunately, just since 2009, we have seen major usurpations against these vital constitutional guarantees. We'll discuss the specific changes since 2009 just ahead. But first, it is amazing that there has been little concern voiced in the media or among the American citizenry. When we let our freedoms slip away without a fight or even without concern, we take freedom, prosperity, and happiness away from our posterity. What kind of people do that?

Are we such a people? Each of us must answer this question for himself. Moreover, the loss of these vital constitutional foundations is not an issue of parties—most liberals, conservatives, environmentalists, radicals, extremists, moderates, hawks, doves, independents, and nearly everyone else are generally opposed to losing our freedoms. So why do we sit by and let it just happen?

The answer is simple, though the reality is quite complex: We tend to let our freedoms slip away because they are tucked away in documents and policies that most of us don't ever read or deal with directly. We either ignore current bills before Congress or, if we do get involved, we focus on the pub-

> *We tend to let our freedoms slip away because they are tucked away in documents and policies that most of us don't ever read or deal with directly.*

licized issues instead of the many layers of complexity. In short, as a nation, we don't read the fine print. Canada and many free nations have the same problem.

The Power of the Fine Print

Many people ignore the fine print in their job contracts and mortgage papers; we glibly sign our signatures and trust others to handle the details. And these things directly, personally, and immediately impact our finances and lives! Imagine how lax we are with proposed bills in Washington, D.C., written by someone we don't know and voted on by people few of us will ever even meet.

What we don't seem to realize is that these things have a direct and major impact on our lives. Our freedoms erode right under our noses, and few of us notice until it is too late. The problem in modern America is not that an individual can't make a difference, but that nearly all of us are too distracted to even try.

> *The problem in modern America is not that an individual can't make a difference, but that nearly all of us are too distracted to even try.*

Perhaps it seems ridiculous to suggest that regular people should read the fine print of proposed legislation and existing laws and court cases and try to improve them. It may even sound extreme to suggest that without such close scrutiny from the citizens, our freedoms will be lost. But it is true. This is one of the things which makes the American founding generations so truly amazing.

Yes, they sacrificed greatly in the Revolution. But many nations have sacrificed mightily and still failed to be free. Yes, the founders wanted to protect themselves from the usurpations of Britain. But so has pretty much every other colony and group of people facing a dominating government. Yes, the founders loved freedom and wanted to pass it on to their children and posterity. But who doesn't?

Almost every human society has wanted to be free. But the American founding generations did something that almost no others have ever done. They read the fine print! They taught their children to read bills, laws, court cases, legislative debates, executive decrees, and bureaucratic policies.

> *The American founding generations did something that almost no others have ever done. They read the fine print!*

They read them in schoolrooms and at home. They read them at picnics and by candlelight after a long and hard day's labor. They said they would consider their children uneducated if they didn't read such things.

In fairness to most human societies who wanted to be free, the regular people through much of history couldn't read at all. The founders understood this, so the first federal law passed under the newly ratified U.S. Constitution (the Northwest Ordinance) required any territory seeking statehood to show that it had an effective educational offering for all children. They considered it a great blessing of providence that they could read and had the chance to pass on education to nearly all citizens.

A Requirement for Freedom

They saw this as a fundamental requirement for freedom, and they mourned for the many generations of humans through history who had no chance at freedom because they simply had no way of getting educated.

But what would the founders think of three generations of today's Americans who can read, who live in relative affluence and have ample leisure time, but who choose to basically ignore most government documents? I think they would be shocked, and then angry.

After the painful price they paid to establish a free nation—the many sacrifices of their families and lives—imagine their frustration that we won't even *read* what the government is doing. Eventually, after their anger wore off, I think they would resign themselves to the following reality: Unless we start reading government documents again (from history and also from current events), we will lose our freedom.

Again, if this sounds extreme, remember that the founding generations read government documents in detail from all three branches and all levels of government from federal to state to local, and they raised their children to do the same. It was second nature to them because they wanted to remain free.

Free people read the fine print. Then they act on it. Those who don't simply do not remain free. This is the reality of history, from Ancient Israel to the Greeks, Saracens, Franks, Anglo-Saxons, and every other free society in history. There are no exceptions in written history. In fact, in places where only the upper classes read government documents, like in Athens or the Roman Republic, only the upper classes were free citizens.

Four Tragedies

As I mentioned earlier, in just the few years since 2009, we have seen four of the major vital foundations of constitutional freedom ignored. People who don't read government documents, or at the very least printed media reports about government documents, aren't even aware of these huge crashes in our constitutional system. They have no idea of the tragedy ahead unless these things are reversed.

Moreover, people who don't read government documents are often swayed by the anger of politicians or media so that they think breaking the Constitution is okay if the nation is mad enough. For example, the vital constitutional foundation of "no bills of attainder" was broken in the wake of national anger at Wall Street after the economic meltdown of 2008-2009. Even some who knew it was broken felt it was justified given Wall Street's mistakes.

But when we let the government break the Constitution because we are really mad, we will soon watch it break the Constitution when we are not mad. This is reminiscent of the old story of many Germans ignoring Hitler's men when they took the Jews, then ignoring them when they took all foreigners, and then ignoring them when they took the white-collar professionals, only to wonder why nobody helped them when Hitler's men came to *their* houses.

Freedom lasts when we stand up for any group unjustly attacked. That is the character of people who will remain free. As Martin Luther King, Jr., said, "Injustice anywhere is a threat to justice everywhere."

> *Freedom lasts when we stand up for any group unjustly attacked.*

Because we were so angry at Wall Street after the economic crisis, we also ignored (or just accepted) the *ex post facto* laws unconstitutionally passed in 2009. That's two strikes against the Constitution, and in less than a year!

The third strike came in the health care law passed under President Barack Obama. Whether you tend to be conservative or progressive, the undeniable reality is that the fine print in the law struck a major blow to one of the most vital foundations of the Constitution.

Specifically, the Constitution separated the powers of the federal government from others that would be left to the states or lower levels. This is as fundamental to our freedoms as separating the executive, judicial, and legislative branches or outlining specific checks and balances.

Take away this provision of separating state and federal powers, and the whole Constitution is in danger of failing. The founding generation felt so strongly about this that they insisted on adding the Ninth and Tenth Amendments to protect this separation and maintain states' rights. Yet today, many citizens haven't read the fine print in these vitally important amendments.

Later, the Supreme Court ruled that the federal government could take some actions within states under the commerce clause, but only the states had the right to require individual citizens to buy a good or service.

In *Gonzales v. Oregon*, the court ruled that the federal government does not have the authority to "define general standards of medical practice in every locality." It also "has recognized a right to medical self-determination, notably finding it within the Fifth Amendment's due process clause."

The Obama-led health care law was the first federal law to break these, and it set a dangerous precedent for the future. In short, under this model, U.S. presidents and Congress can add one or two sentences in any bill at any time that requires Americans to do or buy anything—and pretty much nobody is likely to know until the law is passed.

A fourth blow to freedom came in 2012 when the U.S. adopted the National Defense Authorization Act, which allows military personnel to arrest and hold American citizens in indefinite incarceration without warrant, charges, or trial. The goal of this law was to stop terrorism, but it can be used against anyone the government decides to label a possible terrorist—without court oversight or any of the requirements of due process listed in the first ten amendments of the Constitution.

The pace of such changes to our freedoms seems to be increasing, and few Americans are reading the fine print or paying attention to these sweeping alterations of our constitutional system.

The Only Overseers of Freedom

Some might argue that our elected representatives should keep an eye on such things and take care of them for us. Unfortunately, however, our elected officials often fail to do anything about these fine-print decreases of our freedoms.

Sometimes, even when such things are taken out of legislation by our representatives, the agencies which implement these laws simply write them back into their operating policies and enforce them anyway—even though they are not technically law.

The people can take notice of this and require it to change, but there has been little such widespread involvement in modern times. The people are the only true overseers of freedom. If we don't do it, freedom will be lost.

> The people are the only true overseers of freedom.

For example, the changes in 1913 could have been stopped if enough citizens had been reading the fine print. Unfortunately, this didn't happen, and the Turning Point away from freedom came and went with hardly any opposition from the American people. The *Butler* decision in 1936 was similarly ignored by nearly everyone in the United States, so no pressure was put on Congress or anyone else to respond to this major loss of freedom.

It is up to the people to safeguard freedom. Nobody else is going to do this for us. This is why the founding generations read resolutions, bills, laws, policies, executive orders, ordinances, court cases, and judicial commentaries on cases—as part of their daily reading.

They wanted to be free, so they did what free people always do: They read the documents of government. They studied the fine print. And where they saw dangers to freedom, they took action.

Unfortunately in our time, too often any criticism of one party's policy is interpreted by people as an attack on that party. In this case, it is not my purpose to only criticize President Obama's push for health care reform. I am simply concerned with the way this law treats the U.S. Constitution. Presidents Nixon, Ford, Carter, Reagan, Bush, Clinton, and Bush also promoted policies that threatened constitutional principles.

It is the role of practical politicians to promote policies and changes they feel are needed, and at times these push the envelope of the Constitution. It is up to the people to oversee all this and keep the government from abusing its power. If anyone deserves criticism for our modern loss of freedom, it is us, the people.

Congress and the court must of course do their constitutional role of analyzing and responding to such proposals, but ultimately it is up to the people to protect freedom.

Societies where the regular people aren't allowed to read or comment on the laws are totalitarian, authoritarian, or dictatorial. Societies where the regular people are allowed to read and comment on the government and laws but instead decide not to, leaving it mostly to others, end up losing their freedoms. Most end up adopting Aristocracy or Socialism.

If we want to be free, we must read the fine print.

CHAPTER 13

The Last Turning Point

"The majority of men meet with failure because
of their lack of persistence."
—Napoleon Hill

Freedom only lasts in societies whose regular citizens read government documents, think about and discuss them, do something to change them when needed, and teach their children to do the same. If we become such people, the future of freedom and prosperity is bright. If not…it isn't.

Unfortunately for us, few citizens have done this over time. Few closely studied the Sixteenth or Seventeenth Amendments, the establishment of the Federal Reserve, or the consequences of the *Butler* case. The impact on our society has been a significant loss of freedom.

The last Turning Point, from 1913 to 1936, moved our society away from freedom in the direction of increased force. We are now witnessing many consequences of this major historical shift.

The next great Turning Point is still ahead. Our generation will choose whether we move our society drastically in the direction of more force or more freedom. This change will be led by those who prepare themselves for leadership through voracious reading, independent thinking, building communities, and entrepreneurial success.

All indications are that twenty-five years from now, we will be reaping the consequences of another major Turning Point that is still ahead of us today. We will choose more freedom or less freedom, prosperity or an opportunity-killing class system, a new American century or something much less desirable. It is up to us.

More to the point, we are making these choices each day. Our choices to read or not to read, to get actively involved in our community and government or not, and to build successful businesses or leave such leadership to others are creating our future—one choice at a time.

The Next Shift

Another Turning Point is coming. If we follow the patterns of history, only a few will know about it when it happens, and only a few will be prepared to make a significant influence on what direction it takes.

If we could travel back in time to 1913, perhaps many of us would take action to change the way things turned out. Would we read more and be prepared to speak out effectively against the three great changes of 1913? Would we carefully study the fine print to understand when these three changes were being decided? Would we build communities and businesses of influence to help change these three decisions?

All of that is in the past, and none of us have the power to go back and change these things. But we do have the ability (some would say *duty*) to do these things now, today, in our time.

Freedom matters. Author Rod Stryker wrote that each person has four overarching desires in this life:

1.   A life of purpose
2.   Happiness
3.   Prosperity
4.   Freedom

Without freedom, the other three are much more difficult. Freedom makes purpose and prosperity possible, and it greatly enhances each person's pursuit of happiness.

Freedom matters. A Turning Point is coming. It will either reboot freedom or further diminish our freedoms and prosperity. A few in our generation will make this choice. It is up to us to prepare and become part of this group to ensure that freedom wins the day.

And *now* is the time to act. Three small but important things will make all the difference in each person's preparation to lead: becoming a leader, voracious reading and independent thinking, and building a successful community and/or business.

In Our Hands

The future of freedom is in our hands. If we could look ahead fifty years and see the consequences of our choices now, would we see the vital importance of doing these simple things that will make all the difference? Would we witness a world less free or a society of abundant opportunity and prosperity?

One thing is certain: Without freedom, the future is bleak, and our choices in the months and years ahead will have a direct impact on the future of freedom. It is said that people only really understand freedom once they have lost it. Hopefully, we will be wiser than this.

> *It is said that people only really understand freedom once they have lost it. Hopefully, we will be wiser than this.*

When Allen Bloom ended his best-selling book *The Closing of the American Mind,* he predicted that our future is surely one of increasing decline. In contrast, I am an optimist, and I believe that the best America and freedom have to offer the world is still ahead. But it will depend less on Washington than on our regular citizens. As a people, we will decide our future.

We will be led by those who put a priority on voracious reading, independent thinking, study of the fine print, deep consideration of the great classics of mankind, and taking action as leaders to build communities and businesses.

The leaders of the future are in our homes today. It is time for each of us to put aside our fears, insecurities, weaknesses, and road-blocks and to rise to our potential. It is time to go to work becoming better leaders and building leadership communities.

It is my conviction that we were born for this. Our generation is here for such a time as this—to win the battle for freedom and prosperity for all.

For the American founders, this battle cost blood, life, and massive sacrifice. The same price was asked of the Civil War, World War I, and World War II generations.

For us, thankfully, doing our part simply requires us to rise to our true potential. There are great classics to read, important documents to be studied, and businesses to build. These things will literally change the future. We are up to the task, but we must get to work.

It is time, right now, to get started. The future of freedom hangs in the balance....

Recommended Readings

- Acton, Lord John, *Essays on Freedom and Power*
- Acton, Lord John, *Essays in the History of Liberty*
- Adler, Mortimer J., 2003, *Annals of America*, 22 volumes
- Adler, Mortimer J., 1952, *Great Books of the Western World*, 54 volumes
- Adler, Mortimer J., 1952, *The Great Ideas: A Lexicon of Western Thought*
- Allen, W.B., 1988, *George Washington: A Collection*
- Aristotle, *Politics*
- Auerswald, Philip, 2012, *The Coming Prosperity: How Entrepreneurs are Transforming the Global Economy*
- Aurelius, *Meditations*
- Bacon, Francis, *Advancement of Learning*
- Bastiat, Frederic, 1850, *Economic Harmonies*
- Bastiat, Frederic, 1845, *Economic Sophisms*
- Bastiat, Frederic, 1850, *The Law*
- Bastiat, Frederic, 1848, *Selected Essays on Political Economy*

- Benton, Thomas Hart, 1831, "The Mischiefs of a National Bank"
- Bergh, Albert Ellery, 1907, *The Writings of Thomas Jefferson,* 20 volumes
- Bergsten, C. Fred, et al., 2009, *China's Rise: Challenges and Opportunities*
- Bergsten, C. Fred, 1996, *Dilemmas of the Dollar: The Economics and Politics of United States International Monetary Policy*
- Berlin, Isaiah, 1969, *Two Concepts of Liberty*
- Black, Henry Campbell, 1990, *Black's Law Dictionary*
- Blackstone, William, *Commentaries on the Laws of England,* 4 volumes
- Bloom, Allan, 1987, *The Closing of the American Mind*
- Bloom, Allan, 1996, *Shakespeare's Politics*
- Bloom, Harold, 1994, *The Western Canon*
- Bobbitt, Phillipp, 2002, *The Shield of Achilles: War, Peace, and the Course of History*
- Brady, Chris, 2010, *Rascal: Making a Difference By Becoming an Original Character*
- Brooks, David, 2011, *The Paradise Suite: Bobos in Paradise and On Paradise Drive*
- Bryce, James, 1889, *The American Commonwealth*, 2 volumes
- Brzezinski, Zbigniew, 1998, *The Grand Chessboard*
- Burke, Edmund, *Reflections on the Revolution in France*
- Calvin, John, *Institutes of the Christian Religion*
- Carey, George W., ed., 2000, *The Political Writings of John Adams*

- Carson, Clarence, 1970, *The American Tradition*
- Carson, Clarence, 1995, *A Basic History of the United States,* 6 volumes
- Cicero, *Laws*
- Cicero, *Republic*
- Codevilla, Angelo M., 1997, *The Character of Nations: How Politics Makes and Breaks Prosperity, Family and Civility*
- "Conference on a Stable Dollar: Why We Need it and How to Get It," Heritage Foundation, October 5-6, 2011
- *Constitution of the United States of America*
- Coolidge, Calvin, 1924, *The Price of Freedom*
- Cooper, James Fenimore, 1838, *The American Democrat*
- *Declaration of Independence*
- DeMille, Oliver, 2000, *A Thomas Jefferson Education*
- DeMille, Oliver, 2009, *The Coming Aristocracy: Education and the Future of Freedom*
- DeMille, Oliver, 2010, *FreedomShift: 3 Choices to Reclaim America's Destiny*
- Dickinson, John, 1767, *Letters from a Farmer in Pennsylvania*
- Durant, Will and Ariel, 1968, *The Lessons of History*
- Durant, Will and Ariel, 1935-1975, *The Story of Civilization,* 11 volumes
- Eastman, John C., "Enough is Enough: Why General Welfare Limits Spending," January 13, 2011
- Ebenstein, William, 1963, *Great Political Thinkers*
- Eichengreen, Barry, "When Currencies Collapse: Will We

Replay the 1930s or the 1970s?", *Foreign Affairs,* January/ February, 2012

- Eliot, Charles W., 1909, *The Harvard Classics,* 50 volumes
- Elliot, Jonathan, ed., 1901, *The Debates in the Several State Constitutions on the Adoption of the Federal Constitution*
- Emerson, Ralph Waldo, *Self-Reliance and Other Essays*
- Epictetus, *Discourses*
- Farrand, Max, 1974, *Records of the Federal Convention of 1787*
- Ferguson, Niall, 2011, *Civilization: The West and the Rest*
- Fitzpatrick, John C., ed., 1931-1944, *The Writings of George Washington,* 39 volumes
- Frieden, Jeffry, 2007, *Global Capitalism: Its Fall and Rise in the Twentieth Century*
- Friedman, Thomas L., 2007, *The World is Flat 3.0*
- Friedman, Thomas L. and Michael Mandelbaum, 2011, *That Used to Be Us: How America Fell Behind in the World It Invented and How We Can Come Back*
- Fukuyama, Francis, 2007, *America at the Crossroads: Democracy, Power, and the Neoconservative Legacy*
- Gibbon, Edward, 1776, *The Decline and Fall of the Roman Empire,* 6 volumes
- Gilpin, Robert and Jean M., 2001, *Global Political Economy: Understanding the International Economic Order*
- Gregg, Gary L. II, ed., 1999, *Vital Remnants*
- Grun, Bernard, 2005, *The Timetables of History*

- Guelzo, Allen, "Abraham Lincoln or the Progressives: Who Was the Real Father of Big Government," *Heritage Foundation Special Report*, February 10, 2012
- Hall, Kermit L. and Mark David Hall, eds., 2007, *Collected Works of James Wilson*, 2 volumes
- Hall, Kermit L., ed., et al., 1992, *Oxford Companion to the Supreme Court of the United States*
- Hamilton, Alexander, 1791, "For the Bank"
- Hayek, F.A., 1960, *The Constitution of Liberty*
- Hazlitt, Henry, 1962, *Economics in One Lesson*
- Herodotus, *The Histories*
- Hobbes, Thomas, *Leviathan*
- Homer, *Odyssey*
- Hume, David, 1777, *Essays Moral, Political and Literary*
- Huntington, Samuel P., 1996, *The Clash of Civilizations and the Remaking of World Order*
- Hyneman, Charles and Donald S. Lutz, 1983, *American Political Writings During the Founding Era 1760-1805*, 2 volumes
- Jackson, Andrew, 1932, "Veto Message of the Bank Renewal Bill"
- Jefferson, Thomas, 1791, "Against the Bank"
- Johnson, Paul, 1997, *A History of the American People*
- Keohane, Robert O., 2005, *After Hegemony: Cooperation and Discord in the World Political Economy*
- Keohane, Robert O., 2011, *Power and Independence*
- Kennedy, Paul, 1987, *The Rise and Fall of the Great Powers*

- Ketchum, Ralph, 1986, *The Anti-Federalist Papers and the Constitutional Convention Debates*
- Keynes, John Maynard, 1936, *The General Theory of Employment Interest and Money*
- Kirk, Russell, 1951, *John Randolph of Roanoke: A Study in American Politics*
- Kirk, Russell, 1991, *The Roots of American Order*
- Kissinger, Henry, 1995, *Diplomacy*
- Kissinger, Henry, 2011, *On China*
- Koch, Adrienne, ed., 1965, *The American Enlightenment*
- Kurland, Philip B. and Ralph Lerner, 1987, *The Founders' Constitution*, 5 volumes
- Lee, Richard Henry, 1787, *Letters from the Federal Farmer*
- Legro, Jeffrey W., 2007, *Rethinking the World: Great Power Strategies and International Order*
- Locke, John, *Two Treatises of Government*.
- Leckie, Robert, 1992, *The Wars of America*, 2 volumes
- Lewis, Nathan, 2007, *Gold: The Once and Future Money*
- Lodge, Henry Cabot, 1904, *The Works of Alexander Hamilton*, 12 volumes
- Luther, Martin, *A Treatise on Christian Liberty*
- Lutz, Donald S., 1998, *Colonial Origins of the American Constitution*
- Madison, James and Alexander Hamilton and John Jay, 1789, *The Federalist*
- Marx, Karl, 1867, *Das Kapital*

- Marx, Karl and Friedrich Engels, 1848, *The Communist Manifesto*
- McCreal, Ian P., 1992, *Great Thinkers of the Western World*
- McCullough, David G., 2006, *1776*
- McCullough, David G., 1993, *Truman*
- McDonald, Forest, 1982, *A Constitutional History of the United States*
- McDowell, Gary and Edwin Meese III, "The Language of Law and the Foundations of American Constitutionalism," April 11, 2011
- Meese, Edwin, et al., eds., 2005, *The Heritage Guide to the Constitution*
- Mill, J.S., 1859, *On Liberty*
- Miller, Marion M., 1913, "Direct vs. Indirect Taxation: Debates in the House of Representatives," *Great Debates in American History*, 14 volumes, v. 12, ch. I
- Miller, Marion M., 1913, "The Income Tax: Debates in the House of Representatives and the Senate, and on the Constitutional Amendment," *Great Debates in American History*, 14 volumes, v. 12, ch. XVII
- Miller, Marion M., 1913, "Popular Elections: Debate in the Senate on Popular Elections of Senators," *Great Debates in American History*, 14 volumes, v. 9, ch. XII
- Mises, Ludwig Von, 1949, *Human Action: A Treatise on Economics*
- Monroe, James, 1823, "The Monroe Doctrine"

- Montesquieu, Charles de, *The Spirit of the Laws*
- Naisbitt, John, 1982, *Megatrends: Ten New Directions Transforming Our Lives*
- Naisbitt, John and Doris, 2010, *China's Megatrends: The 8 Pillars of a New Society*
- Naisbitt, John, 2008, *Mindset!: Eleven Ways to Change the Way You See—and Create—the Future*
- Nowak, John E., and Ronald D. Rotunda, 2004, *Constitutional Law*, Seventh Edition
- Nye, Joseph S. Jr., 2011, *The Future of Power*
- Padover, Saul K., 1953, *The Complete Madison*
- Paine, Thomas, *The Rights of Man*
- Peck, Don, 2011, *Pinched: How the Great Recession Has Narrowed Our Futures and What We Can Do About It*
- Pink, Daniel H., 2006, *A Whole New Mind: Why Right-Brainers Will Rule the Future*
- Pink, Daniel H., 2011, *Drive: The Surprising Truth About What Motivates*
- Plato, *Dialogues of Plato*, Translated by Benjamin Jowett
- Plato, *The Republic*, Translated by Benjamin Jowett
- Plato, *Seventh Letter*
- Plotinus, *Sixth Ennead*
- Plutarch, *Lives of the Noble Greeks and Romans*
- Polybius, *Histories*
- Postman, Neil, 1985, *Amusing Ourselves to Death*
- Quigley, Carrol, 1979, *The Evolution of Civilizations*

- Quigley, Carrol, 1975, *Tragedy & Hope: A History of the World in Our Time*
- Rothbard, Murray, 1963, *America's Great Depression*
- Rothbard, Murray, 1962, *Man, Economy and the State*
- Rutland, Robert A., 1962, *The Papers of James Madison*
- Sandoz, Ellis, 1998, *Political Sermons of the American Founding Era, 1730-1805*, 2 volumes
- Schick, Allen, 2007, *The Federal Budget: Politics, Policy, Process,* Third Edition
- Shakespeare, William, *Coriolanus*
- Shakespeare, William, *Henry VI*
- Shakespeare, William, *Julius Caesar*
- Shakespeare, William, *Richard III*
- Shapiro, Gary, 2011, *The Comeback: How Innovation Will Restore the American Dream*
- Sheehan, Colleen A. and Gary A. McDowell, eds., 1998, *Friends of the Constitution: Writings of the "Other" Federalists 1787-1788*
- Sidney, Algernon, *Discourses on Government*
- Skousen, W. Cleon, 1981, *The Five Thousand Year Leap*
- Skousen, W. Cleon, 1985, *The Making of America*
- Smith, Adam, *The Wealth of Nations*
- Smyth, Albert Henry, 1905-1907, *The Writings of Benjamin Franklin,* 10 volumes
- Solzhenitsyn, Aleksandr, 1978, *A World Split Apart*
- Solzhenitsyn, Aleksandr, *The Gulag Archipelago*—the Thom-

as P. Whitney and Harry Willets translation as abridged and edited by Edward E. Ericson, Jr., published in 2002 by HarperCollins

- Story, Joseph, 1858, *Commentaries on the Constitution of the United States,* 2 volumes
- Strauss, Leo and Joseph Cropsey, eds., 1963, *History of Political Philosophy*
- Strauss, William and Neil Howe, 1997,*The Fourth Turning*
- Strong, Michael, 2009, *Be the Solution: How Entrepreneurs and Conscious Capitalists Can Solve All the World's Problems*
- Tacitus, *Annals*
- Thomas, C. Bradley, 2000, *The Revolutionary Writings of John Adams*
- Thucydides, *History of the Peloponnesian Wars*
- Tocqueville, Alexis, 1847, *Democracy in America.* (I prefer the Henry Reeve text as revised by Francis Bowen, edited by Phillips Bradley, and published by Alfred A. Knopf.)
- Toffler, Alvin, 1981, *The Third Wave*
- Toffler, Alvin, 2007, *Revolutionary Wealth*
- Toynbee, Arnold J., 1946, *A Study of History*
- Tucker, St. George, 1803, *View of the Constitution of the United States*
- Virgil, *Georgics*
- Virgil, *Aeneid*
- Walker, Timothy, 1837, *Introduction to American Law*
- Washington, George, 1789, "First Inaugural Address"

- Washington, George, 1796, "Farewell Address"
- Webster, Noah, 1828, *American Dictionary of the English Language*
- Wilson, Woodrow, 1913, "Inaugural Address"
- Wood, Gordon S., 2011, *The Idea of America: Reflections on the Birth of the United States*
- Woodward, Orrin, 2011, *Resolved: 13 Resolutions for LIFE*
- Woodward, Orrin and Chris Brady, 2008, *Launching a Leadership Revolution: Mastering the Five Levels of Influence*
- Zakaria, Fareed, 2011, *The Post-American World: Release 2.0*

Notes

Introduction

See *The Annals of America* by Mortimer J. Adler, volume 13, pages 412-415 for further commentary on President Wilson's policies.

Chapter 1

See *Federalist Papers* 18-20 for historical examples of seemingly insignificant events that changed the course of history.

See Joseph Nye's argument about our being "addicted to bad policies" in his November/December 2010 *Foreign Affairs* article, "The Future of American Power: Dominance and Decline in Perspective."

Chapter 2

While some have argued that the Sixteenth Amendment was never properly ratified, the reality is that the nation has operated under its provisions since 1913.

For more details on the founders' perspective on taxation, see *A History of the American People* by Paul Johnson, pages 13-14 and 21.

See *Letters from a Farmer in Pennsylvania* by founding father John Dickinson for more information on early proposals that America should remain part of the British Empire and subject to the King as long as each American colony was governed by its own parliament.

See *Federalist Papers* 21, 33, 34, 35, 36, and 41 for more information on why indirect taxes are essential to freedom and direct taxes are dangerous.

For more information on the twenty enumerated powers in the Constitution, see *The Making of America* by W. Cleon Skousen, pages 371-464.

The Supreme Court struck down the 1894 income tax law passed by Congress in *Pollock v. Farmers' Loan & Trust Co.*, 1895. Also see *The Oxford Companion to the Supreme Court of the United States* by Kermit Hall, et al, pages 654-655, and *A Defence of the Constitutions of the Government of the United States of America* by John Adams, as quoted in *The Political Writings of John Adams* by George W. Carey, pages 115-116.

Chapter 4

There were actually several national bank acts between 1863-1864, and these came after the Second National Bank and before the Federal Reserve and could be referred to as "Third National Banks."

For more information on the history of government coinage, see *De Moneta*, written in the mid-1300s, by Nicholas Oresme, as cited in *Gold: The Once and Future Money* by Nathan Lewis, page 71. Lewis' book is an excellent historical analysis of sound money and lesser money. Also see *The Wealth of Nations* by Adam Smith.

When people speak of the "gold standard," a more accurate term might be the "silver standard," since sound money systems usually implement more silver exchange and currency than merely gold.

See *The Making of America* by W. Cleon Skousen, pages 423-424 for more information on criticisms of a national bank and the plan to require all currencies to be redeemable in gold or silver. The book also details the Coinage Act of 1792, which sentenced people who debased the currency to the death penalty.

Read more on inflation in "Inflation and Deflation," by John Maynard Keynes in *Essays in Persuasion*, page 78, as cited in *Gold: The Once and Future Money* by Nathan Lewis, page 73.

Economist Murray Rothbard's views on fiat currency were gleaned from personal discussions and seminar conversations with the author. An excellent book on the topic of gold currency is *Gold: The Once and Future Money* by Nathan K. Lewis.

Items in this section are from Orrin Woodward, 2011, *RE-SOLVED: 13 Resolutions for LIFE*, pp. 290-295. This history is also discussed in Nathan Lewis, 2007, *Gold: The Once and Future Money*, pp. 153-174.

See *The Making of America* by W. Cleon Skousen, pages 423-424, for more information on the phrase "emit bills of credit," which was removed from the Constitution, as well as information on banking and counterfeiting issues during the Civil War.

Note that U.S. citizens were taken off the gold standard in 1933, meaning that they could not redeem U.S. paper currency for gold or silver. Foreigners could redeem U.S. currency for gold or silver until 1973.

Chapter 5

For more information on the *Marbury v. Madison* case, see *The Making of America* by W. Cleon Skousen, page 575, and *Constitutional Law* by John E. Nowak and Ronald D. Rotunda, Seventh Edition, pages 1-21.

For Jefferson's correspondence regarding his views on the Supreme Court, see *The Writings of Thomas Jefferson* by Albert Ellery Bergh, particularly volume 11, pages 50 and 213, and volume 15, pages 212 and 330-332.

For more information on judicial technocracy, see the following court cases: *Cohen v. Commonwealth of Virginia,* 1821; *Gibbons v. Ogden,* 1824; *Missouri v. Holland,* 1920; *U.S. v. Curtiss-Wright Export Corp.,* 1936; *New York ex rel. Cohn v. Graves,* 1937.

Read the court's majority opinion on *United States v. Butler* in *Constitutional Law* by John E. Nowak and Ronald D. Rotunda, Seventh Edition, pages 230-231.

See *The Oxford Companion to the Supreme Court of the United States* by Kermit Hall, et al, pages 111-112 to read Justice Harlan Stone's rebuttal in the *Butler* case, and for more information on the court's opinions regarding "general welfare."

See Sandra Day O'Connor's dissent of *South Dakota v. Dole,* 1987 for commentary on the court's decisions since the *Butler* case.

For more information on the federal budget increasing after the *Butler* case, see *The Making of America* by W. Cleon Skousen, page 255.

Chapter 6

The concept of principles (truths that are universal and the foundation of all wisdom and practical application) was widely believed in the founding era, but is less so today. For a commentary on the influence of a core belief in principles through the history of Western Civilization, see *The Great Ideas: A Syntopicon of Great Books of the Western World* by Mortimer J. Adler, chapter 71.

See *The Five Thousand Year Leap* by W. Cleon Skousen, pages 11-19, for more information regarding government practices by the ancient Israelites and the Anglo-Saxons.

John Adams' thoughts on early American education are found in *The American Enlightenment* by Adrienne Koch and are cited in *The Five Thousand Year Leap* by W. Cleon Skousen, page 250.

Read Alexis de Tocqueville's thoughts on early American education in *Democracy in America* (Vintage Edition, 1945), volume 1, pages 326-327.

See a similar commentary on the education of the American populace just prior to the Civil War in *Amusing Ourselves to Death* by Neil Postman, pages 44-49. Tocqueville portrays a similar culture in the 1830s in *Democracy in America*. (I prefer the Henry Reeve text as revised by Francis Bowen, edited by Phillips Bradley, and published by Alfred A. Knopf.)

See *Federalist Papers* 51 and 63 for more information on auxiliary precautions.

Learn more about Murray Rothbard's seven human interactions in *Man, Economy and the State*, pages 71-80.

An excellent book that shows the reality of the pattern of government's abuse of power over long periods of human history is *Lives of the Noble Greeks and Romans* by Plutarch.

See Madison's comments on the fundamental purposes of government and the reasons we need government (and need it to be limited, checked, and balanced) in *Federalist* 51. Also see *Federalist Papers* 49 and 50.

Chapter 8

A great book on the value of entrepreneurship is *Revolutionary Wealth* by Alvin Toffler.

See Arne Duncan's November/December 2012 *Foreign Affairs* article "Back to School: Enhancing U.S. Education and Competitiveness" for his thoughts on keeping America's economy safe and vibrant.

Chapter 9

Samuel Williams' thoughts are documented in *The Natural and Civil History of Vermont*, a textbook used in Vermont for many years. They are also cited in *American Political Writings During the Founding Era* by Charles S. Hyneman and Donald S. Lutz, volume 2, page 951.

President Coolidge argued that Washington, Hamilton, and Jefferson were indispensable to establishing the Constitution. Without Washington's support, the Constitutional Convention would not have occurred or completed a constitution. Without Jefferson, the constitutional system would not have become nationally popular and accepted. And without Hamilton, the Constitution would not have been ratified since it was Hamilton who pushed the *Federalist* in New York and got the Constitution ratified.

Calvin Coolidge quotes were taken from the following sources:

"The Limitations of Law," Speech to the American Bar Association in San Francisco, California, August 10, 1922. Cited in Calvin Coolidge, 1924, *The Price of Freedom*, 2001 Edition, pp. 199-200.

"The Power of Moral Law," Speech in Springfield, Massachusetts, October 11, 1921. Cited in Calvin Coolidge, 1924, *The Price of Freedom*, 2001 Edition, p. 72.

"Our Heritage from Hamilton," Speech in Chicago, Illinois, January 11, 1922. Cited in Calvin Coolidge, 1924, *The Price of Freedom*, 2001 Edition, p. 99.

"The Destiny of America," Speech in Northampton, Massachusetts, May 30, 1923. Cited in Calvin Coolidge, 1924, *The Price of Freedom*, 2001 Edition, p. 329.

"The Title of American," Speech in Kansas City, Missouri, October 31, 1921. Cited in Calvin Coolidge, 1924, *The Price of Freedom*, 2001 Edition, p. 96.

"The Limitations of the Law," Speech to the American Bar Association in San Francisco, California, August 10, 1922. Cited in Calvin Coolidge, 1924, *The Price of Freedom*, 2001 Edition, p. 196.

"The Foundation of Our Institutions," Speech in Albany, New York, April 12, 1923. Cited in Calvin Coolidge, 1924, *The Price of Freedom*, 2001 Edition, p. 292.

"The Things That Are Unseen," Speech at Wheaton College, June 19, 1923. Cited in Calvin Coolidge, 1924, *The Price of Freedom*, 2001 Edition, pp. 390-391.

"The Instruments of Progress," Speech at the American University, June 7, 1922. Cited in Calvin Coolidge, 1924, *The Price of Freedom*, 2001 Edition, p. 161.

"Great Virginians," Speech in Fredericksburg, Virginia, July 6, 1922. Cited in Calvin Coolidge, 1924, *The Price of Freedom*, 2001 Edition, p. 174.

Statistics on cultural literacy taken from the following sources:

Les Krantz and Chris Smith, 2011, *The Unofficial U.S. Census*, p. 175.

"Harper's Index," *Harper's Magazine,* March 2012.

World Demographics Profile 2011, Index Mundi.

The Dominion Institute, 2007, "The Canadian History Report Card: Curriculum Analysis in High Schools across Canada."

Kristina R. Llewellyn, et al., "The State and Potential of Civic Learning in Canada: Charting the Cause for Youth Civic and Political Participation," 2007, Canadian Policy Research Networks.

For more information on the evolution and "dumbing down" of American textbooks, see *Dumbing Us Down* by John Taylor Gatto and *Lies My Teacher Told Me: Everything Your American History Textbook Got Wrong* by James W. Loewen.

Chapter 10

The shift away from leaders being mostly landowners and merchants has coincided with a decrease in widespread land ownership in the world. See, for example, *Who Owns the World: The Surprising Truth about Every Piece of Land on the Planet* by Kevin Cahill.

For more information on the leadership revolution, see *Leaders: Strategies for Taking Charge* by Warren Bennis and *Principle-Cen-*

tered Leadership by Stephen R. Covey.

For further reading on local and tribal government and tribal leadership, see:

God's New Israel by Conrad Cherry, pages 1-123.

The Majesty of God's Law by W. Cleon Skousen, pages 11-29.

The writings of Arnold Toynbee and the multi-volume *History of Civilization* by Will & Ariel Durant.

Democracy in America by Alexis de Tocqueville. (I prefer the Henry Reeve text as revised by Francis Bowen, edited by Phillips Bradley, and published by Alfred A. Knopf, v. 1, ch. 5.)

Colonial Origins of the American Constitution by Donald S. Lutz.

Launching a Leadership Revolution: Mastering the Five Levels of Influence by Orrin Woodward and Chris Brady.

Chapter 11

Aristotle discusses primary and secondary qualities in *On the Soul, On Sense and the Sensible*, and *Nichomachean Ethics*, and he comments on freedom at length in *Politics*. Plato also discusses primary and lesser goods in *Timaeus*. John Locke gives a great deal of commentary on this topic in *An Essay Concerning Human Understanding*, and David Hume does the same in *An Enquiry Concerning Human Understanding*. Also see Mortimer Adler, 1952, *The Great Ideas: A Syntopicon of Great Books of the Western World*, ch. 3, 11, 12, 16, 31, 47, 59, 62, 75, 87. Also see the *Declaration of Independence*.

This combination of three kinds of freedom (political, spiritual, and financial) is the major foundation of Western Civilization, as promoted in: the two capitals of the West, Jerusalem and Athens; the two great martyrs of the West, Jesus Christ and Socrates; and the two great classics of Western culture, the Bible and the dialogues of Socrates. For additional commentary on these themes, see Russell Kirk, 1991, *The Roots of American Order.* Note that Jerusalem (like Constantinople) is considered part of the West in some eras of history and part of the Orient, or East, specifically the Near East, in other historical periods.

Regarding the estimated total number of people who have enjoyed freedom, mathematician Carl Haub estimated in 2002 that there have been 106 billion people over the course of the earth's history ("How Many People Have Ever Lived On Earth?," *Population Today,* November/December 2002, Population Reference Bureau). Using this estimate, the number of people living on earth in 2002 made up approximately 6 percent of all the people who have ever lived. In 2002, the year of the mathematical estimate, approximately 9.5 percent of the people in the world lived in nations with relative freedom, which accounted for .0057 percent of the long-term world population. However, if we use the benefits outlined in *The Declaration of Independence* as a definition of "freedom," the number of people who were free according to this standard is significantly reduced. Also, using this same definition, most "free" nations in history and today have only allowed a small number of the upper (and, in a few nations, middle) classes to enjoy the benefits of freedom.

Economic Nobel Laureates Carl Becker and Milton Friedman, along with a team of economists, created the Fraser Index to formally measure world levels of economic freedom. Their five categories of measurement include: 1-Size of Government: Expenditures, Taxes, and Enterprises; 2-Legal Structure and Security of Property Rights; 3-Access to Sound Money; 4-Freedom to Trade Internationally; 5-Regulation of Credit, Labor, and Business. Cited in Michael Strong, 2009, *Be the Solution: How Entrepreneurs and Conscious Capitalists Can Solve All the World's Problems*, pp. 176-183. The third category Sound Money alone justifies the calculation of 1 percent. Categories 1 and 5 further erode the percentage of the calculation, though categories 2 and 4 have made some gains in certain places.

As further evidence of the restriction of freedom, it was widely reported in the news on February 17, 2012 that a child in an American public school took a lunch packed by her mother to school. The lunch included a banana, a turkey sandwich, and apple juice. A teacher at the school inspected all the lunches brought from home, decided that this wasn't an acceptable lunch, and took it away. In replacement, the child was given chicken nuggets from the school's lunch cafeteria. This kind of government intrusion is more and more prevalent even in the relatively free nations. On February 25, 2012, John Stossel reported in *Illegal Everything* the following realities: 1) In many places in the United States, a child setting up a lemonade stand is engaging in an illegal act. In fact, there are numerous cases on the books where the government has shut down lemonade or cookie stands run by children in their front yards; 2) Many people in the U.S. have been fined and threatened with prison because they had a tree in their yard that the government considered the improper kind of tree for the neighborhood—note that in most cases the trees weren't dangerous in any way, just not the kind of tree the government deemed proper; 3) A number of U.S. people holding Bible studies in their homes have been shut down for not having meeting permits from the government. There are many other examples of these kinds of annoying and increasingly abusive actions by governments. Stossel points out that there are 1,000 pages per day of new laws passed in the United States.

Chapter 12

The American founding generations knew how to read the fine print. See *The Natural and Civil History of Vermont* by Samuel Williams, as cited in *American and Political Writings During the Founding Era* by Charles S. Hyneman and Donald S. Lutz, volume 2, page 951.

Information on the *Gonzalez v. Oregon* court case was taken from "Sound and Fury" in the March 20, 2010 edition of *The Economist*.

Chapter 13

Read more on Rod Stryker's "four desires" in *The Four Desires: Creating a Life of Purpose, Happiness, Prosperity and Freedom*.

Other Works by Oliver DeMille

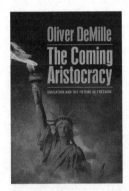

The Coming Aristocracy:
Education and the Future of Freedom

Drawing from years of exhaustive research, Oliver DeMille demonstrates why social, economic, and political equality are being steadily eroded. He highlights crucial constitutional changes, analyzes the current economic crisis, explains why both liberals and conservatives promote aristocracy, and articulates a comprehensive formula for restoring the American republic. *The Coming Aristocracy* is a book for anyone concerned about the decline of America and the steady loss of freedom. More precisely, it is for those dedicated to reversing those trends through education and entrepreneurship.

FreedomShift:
3 Choices to Reclaim America's Destiny

Americans who are so demonstrably willing to labor and sacrifice for the benefit of their posterity can only allow the destruction of the forms that protect our freedoms if they do not understand what freedom is, nor how to maintain it. A

Freedom*Shift* is needed today; and to accomplish it, Oliver DeMille proposes The 3 Choices to Reclaim America's Destiny. *Can it be possible that such a peaceful revolution can be accomplished by three simple choices made by a relative few?*

A Thomas Jefferson Education:
Teaching a Generation of
Leaders for the 21st Century
Is American education preparing the future leaders our nation needs, or merely struggling to teach basic literacy and job skills? Without leadership education, are we settling for an inadequate system that delivers educational, industrial, governmental and societal mediocrity? *A Thomas Jefferson Education* presents a new educational vision based on proven methods that really work! Teachers, students, parents, educators, legislators, leaders and everyone who cares about America's future must read this compelling book.

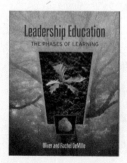

Leadership Education:
The Phases of Learning
(with Rachel DeMille)
This volume continues the Leadership Education Library with a survey of human development research that supports the TJEd philosophy and methodology, plus sections on each of the Phases of Learning: Core,

Love of Learning, Transition to Scholar, Scholar and Depth. In addition, this book illuminates the adult phases of Mission and Impact, with a special Coda on Grandparenting. If you want to implement Leadership Education in your home, school, business or personal life, you will find this an invaluable tool. This inspirational book is considered by many to be the DeMille's best work on education.

A Thomas Jefferson Education
Home Companion
(with Rachel DeMille and Diann Jeppson)
This handy sequel has practical suggestions for helping children progress toward and succeed in the Scholar Phase, including adult skills acquisition, how to conduct a successful family reading time, mentoring tips, club organization helps, how to create a "Momschool", etc.

Thomas Jefferson Education for Teens

(with Shanon Brooks)
This addition to the TJEd library is written to youth and adults wanting to accomplish a successful Scholar Phase–academics, personal development and mission preparation.
It includes: How to find the "Real You"; The **Teen-100 List**; How to study the classics; How to make the most of your mentor; Sample Simulations; ...*plus lots more!*

The Student Whisperer

(with Tiffany Earl)

This book is designed to help you become a great mentor—a true Student Whisperer and leader at the highest level. It will also help you work effectively with such mentors as you pursue your goals and life mission. This book is part deep teaching of the vital principles of great Leadership Education, part self-help workshop, part example through parables, and part exploration of the great ideas that make mentoring and quality learning most effective at all ages.

About the Author

Oliver DeMille is the author of *A Thomas Jefferson Education*, *The Coming Aristocracy* and other books on education and freedom. He is the chairman of The Center for Social Leadership, and he has taught graduate courses on the complete writings of Thomas Jefferson, *The Federalist Papers*, Aristotle's *Politics* and other great classics of liberty. Oliver is a popular keynote speaker, mentor, writer, and business consultant. He is married to the former Rachel Pinegar. They have eight children.

Connect with Oliver at oliverdemille.com
and on Facebook, Twitter, and LinkedIn